Su

D0957461

Survivor

A Woman's Search For Peace

Tania Kauppila

as told to Gene Schrader

THOMAS NELSON PUBLISHERS

Nashville ✳ Camden ✳ New York

Published in Nashville, Tennessee, by Thomas Nelson, Inc. and distributed in Canada by Lawson Falle, Ltd., Cambridge, Ontario.

Printed in the United States of America.

All Scripture quotations are from the New King James Version. Copyright © 1979, 1980, 1982, Thomas Nelson, Inc., Publishers.

Library of Congress Cataloging in Publication Data

Kauppila, Tania.
  Survivor.

  1. Kauppila, Tania. 2. Christian biography—United States. 3. Prisoners of war—Soviet Union—Biography. 4. Prisoners of war—Germany—Biography. 5. World War, 1939-1945—Prisoners and prisons, German. I. Schrader, Gene. II. Title.
BR1725.K346A36 1983   209'.2'4 [B]   83-17330
ISBN 0-8407-5850-2

To my Pastor, Dr. David D. Allen, whose spiritual advice and teaching these many years has helped me "to grow in the grace and knowledge of the Lord Jesus Christ";

To my dear husband Roy, for accepting me—Tania—just as I am; and for granting his permission for his story to be shared, along with mine;

To each of our dearly loved children, and to each of our delightful grandchildren—present and future...

This book is lovingly dedicated.

Tania

---- ✳ ----

Acknowledgments

There are many people whose encouragement, support, and help made this book possible. Any number of ladies have come up to me after I have spoken to a group and said, "Tania, you must write a book." Together, they helped me to see that was indeed the Lord's will. My thanks go to every one of them.

Then there are those good friends who have helped me organize and tell my story. God knows who these wonderful ladies are and will reward them, I am sure, for their kindness, love, and hard work. They have my eternal gratitude.

I must make special mention of Bettylou Tonissen, my good friend, who has done so much work in correcting and updating this book. Without her help it could not have been done, and I am so grateful to her.

Finally I want to thank publicly my husband, Roy, whose encouragement and love have sustained me and given me the freedom to follow the Lord's leading in ministering for His glory.

Contents

1

A Hole in the Ground

---- ✳ ----

"He also brought me up out of a horrible pit" (Ps. 40:2).

We huddled in a hole in the ground—a dirt shelter dug with our own hands—while bullets flew over our heads like whining insects. The light began to grow dim, and the air was choked with smoke. Bombs and shells were exploding all around us. The sound was deafening, and often we screamed in fright as we pressed our bodies tighter against the unyielding dirt. Our fear grew with each moment, with each human shriek that penetrated the sound barrier of battle.

Less than six hours before, our fifteen-year-old neighbor, Vladimir Dmitrenkos, had heard on his radio that the Germans would soon reach the outskirts of our beloved Kiev. After passing the radio message on to us, Vladimir and his twelve-year-old sister, Maruska, hurried breathlessly back to their apartment to help their parents prepare to join our family in the shelter. Everywhere there was shouting, fear, and confusion.

Three weeks earlier, in the dawn of June 22, 1941, German forces had invaded Russia. Many of the major cities on what was later to be known as the Eastern front were bombed. Kiev was one of those cities. And now, in the middle of July, a new, unwanted experience was being thrust upon us, for Kiev was a city under siege.

When the Germans had invaded the Ukraine, the Soviet government had warned, "Prepare a bomb shelter for your family's protection immediately." My father and Vladimir's father lost no time in choosing a spot—an earthen bank about one hundred feet from our houses—and our two families began to feverishly dig the rude shelter. Everyone worked at digging, with a strength born of fear. Even my three-year-old brother, Nicoly (whom we called Kolia), helped to dig.

Now here we were, all eight of us, not knowing how long we would be huddled together: my mother and father, Kolia and I; and our neighbors Vladimir, Maruska, and their mother and father.

Our Russian soldiers fought fiercely. The long hours of the siege stretched into days and weeks. Would it never end? Where would the next shell land? With hearts pounding, we took turns crawling on our stomachs to our houses for water and food and toilet facilities. Each time I returned safely there would be a tearful reunion, and my parents would thank God for His protection over me. I prayed too, while others made their forced journeys, and then cried in thankfulness at the sight of them again.

Once, after an hour of quiet outside, I jumped out to run to the house for water, thinking, *Surely a little girl of eleven will be safe.* However, as soon as I stood up, the bullets cut the air on my right and left sides, and above my head. Even after I entered the building, bullets seeking my life crashed through windows. I flung myself on the floor of the kitchen until it was quiet again. Panic took over, and I was sure I would die and never see my family again. Finally, gulping deep breaths, I opened the door with numb, unfeeling fingers and wormed my way back across the ground, crying out in terror. After what seemed an eternity, I fell exhausted into my mother's arms. Weeping openly, she held me close and whispered comfort and praise for my bravery, and sang a song of gratitude to God.

Gradually the Russian troops were pushed from sector to sector, out of the city. We did not know this, however. We lived on the outskirts in Pushta Wodica, a beautifully wooded semirural subdivision of the city, and the fighting continued longer around us. Once, the eight of us decided to try to follow the retreating Russians. We had heard such horrible reports about our invaders that we were terrified of being captured. When winning the battle seemed hopeless, and the German firepower seemed overwhelmingly the more intense and conquering, all we could think of was escape. We made our plans quickly; at night, when there was a lull in the fighting, we would crawl out of the shelter and head in the direction of the Soviet concentration. We started out over and over again, but each time we tried, it seemed the Germans had advance notice, and heavy crossfire stopped us. We were always forced back into our makeshift, crowded bunker. Toward the end of the offensive, we gave up going out of the shelter at all, except to relieve ourselves at night.

Finally it was over. The German fire was not being returned. Around midnight on September 17, the final pullout of the Russian forces took place, leaving us to the mercy of our enemies. We had been under siege for sixty-four long days and nights.

The Germans quickly occupied every part of the city, and radios and loud-speakers everywhere urged prople not to resist. "We are your friends," they proclaimed in loud, static-interrupted tones. There seemed to be so many of them; they visited every house, every shelter.

At last a guttural command sounded at the entrance to our hideaway, and a rifle was thrust into the opening of our shelter. We knew better than to try to avoid the confrontation, even though we didn't understand what we were to do. We came out of our shelter slowly, cautiously: Father first, then I, then Mama and Kolia, and then our neighbors. The fear in our hearts and the pain in our bodies from the sustained cramped positions were evident in our faces. We practiced walking upright again and glanced about timidly. Familiar landmarks had disappeared. Trees and hills, houses and possessions, had been reduced to common rubble. A shell had destroyed our home. We emerged to a new landscape created by war.

A German soldier motioned for us to move to where a crowd had gathered. An interpreter relayed instructions to us all. The first thing our German "friends" had us do for them was to dig out the parts of the shelters that had caved in. When the Russians came back, the Germans would need these deep holes. As I helped my parents dig, a shovel accidentally cut deep into the nail and flesh of my big toe. "We are your friends," they had said, so I showed them my toe. What an unexpected surprise; they helped me! They cut off the loose flesh and nail, and bandaged me. They gave me medicine, and I was grateful. Without their help, I might have lost that toe. *Germans aren't so bad,* I thought.

Since we had no house to return to, the Dmitrenkoses took us in with them. During the daytime, we began the discouraging job of sifting through the dirt and debris that had once been our home. None of our possessions were to be found. Everything had been destroyed. We had buried a few precious personal treasures outside by the pump in our yard, but those things had been stolen by the hundreds of Russian refugees who now wandered the city. We had nothing but the clothes on our backs at the end of each day's search. Every night we went back to the security of the shelter. Russian mortars occasionally fell in our neighborhood at night, so we felt safer in the shelter during hours.

Keeping our clothing clean was now a problem. We had nothing to wear while my mother busied herself doing our laundry. Fortunately for us, the Dmitrenkoses were able to share from their meager extra clothing. I was glad Maruska was older and larger than I, when it was my turn to have my clothing laundered!

The radio at the Dmitrenkoses' played constantly while we were there. No music or advertising was on the Russian radio; strictly news and announcements. We would hear the Communists telling us not to go with the Germans— not to work for them, or help them in any way in the war effort. "We are Russian comrades. The Germans are the enemy." We heard the Germans saying, "We are your friends."

One morning we heard a radio announcement addressed to the Jewish population in Kiev. A specific date and time were given, when "All Jews are to report to the public square, bringing with you all your personal possessions. Every member of the family is to be there, including grandparents and infants."

We wondered more and more about the announcement as it was repeated periodically throughout that day, and on each succeeding day before the specified date. During one of the announcements, when I noticed my mother's weeping, I questioned her. She just shook her head and said, "Oh, Tania, we are at war, and war is terrible."

My father worked with many Jewish men, and he had told me of their brilliant minds. He also stressed that God loved the Jews dearly, and that His Son Jesus Christ was born of a Jewish mother.

Vladimir, Maruska, and I had already privately decided

that we would be there to see why it was so important for the Jews to be at the public square. We could see other children, apparently as curious as we, headed in the same direction, and we joined them. About thirty of us clustered together, talking excitedly, as children will, wondering what was about to take place. We were no longer under the Russian government, but a new military regime, controlled by the Germans. We wanted to watch the German soldiers to find out what type of people they really were—but we didn't want to get too close, because we did not know exactly what to expect from these men.

"What do you suppose will happen?"

"Do you think they will take them somewhere to work for the Germans in the war effort?"

"How many Jews do you suppose there are—a couple of hundred?"

These and other questions were being asked, usually before anyone had tried to answer the last question.

The area about the square was bustling with activity. Military trucks had been placed end to end on each side of the square, enclosing a large, oblong area. German soldiers with their machine guns were stationed inside the line of trucks. As the Jews arrived, they were ordered to form a single file, and to walk between the double row of soldiers.

Then we heard it begin, the wailing sound coming from the Jewish people. We heard the word, *Fire!* and the wails grew in intensity as the soldiers opened fire with the machine guns. The Jews were caught in a crossfire. There was no escape.

I can still hear in my mind the gunfire and the screams of the people as they fell over into a trench—a trench we hadn't noticed before. Parents clutched their screaming children, and fell together. We were not close enough to distinguish features, but the horror on their faces as they realized the reason for their being there was obvious.

Our terror at first rooted us to the ground. Suddenly, we could bear it no longer. We stopped our ears with our fingers, trying to shut out the sound; and, terrified, ran sobbing from the scene of mass murder. When the three of us finally had to stop to catch our breath, we looked at one another, unable to speak, unable to blot out what we had seen. Home was where we wanted to be. Now I could cry as my mother had cried, and know it firsthand in my own heart: "War is terrible."

Kiev mourned her dead that day. Word spread quickly throughout the city. By evening, everyone knew of the barbaric massacre performed by the German soldiers.

When my parents discovered I had been present at the holocaust, my father scolded me. "Tania! Don't you realize we are at war? A stray bullet might have killed any one of you!" Then he cradled me in his arms, to comfort my fresh storm of tears.

"Why did they do it, Papa? Why? Why?" My father's tears blended with mine, but he just shook his head in sorrow, unable to give me an answer.

Later that night when I should have been asleep, I heard my father whisper to my mother, "Some of them were only wounded, and were still moving in the trenches while the soldiers were covering them with dirt."

"Oh...no!" was my mother's horrified answer.

After a moment or two, my father again whispered in sorrow, "We have lost dear friends today."

With that I turned over and tried to block the memory of the day from my mind. Why had this atrocity been committed against the Jews? There was no way I could justify it. Other fears loomed in my mind: *Could it also happen to us? Would it? Was there safety for anyone in a war? Why had Germany invaded us anyhow? Why couldn't we roll back time and let things be as they were before the war started?* Such were the thoughts of my eleven-year-old mind, as I drifted off into a troubled slumber.

2

Refugees

❊

My times are in Your hand;
Deliver me from the hand of my enemies,
And from those who persecute me (Ps. 31:15).

My wish that things would be as they were before the war began, was not to be. We were poorer than before—no home, no job, no food! The Soviet government was no longer paying my father to build roads and railroads because none were being built. Normal operations would not be resumed for two more years, when the Russians, in a fierce counteroffensive along the entire eastern European front, would recover Kiev. We were destitute.

Soon the Dmitrenkoses' food supply was exhausted, and both of our families joined the hordes of refugee beggars. First we stayed in Kiev, but when its resources seemed gone, we knew we would need to travel farther away, to ask help of our relatives. We said a tearful goodbye to the Dmitrenkoses. They had been such good friends to us. Would we ever see them again?

Transportation as I knew it in Russia, was mostly "footpower." In large cities such as Kiev, streetcars provided transportation to every part of the city, but in smaller villages, everyone walked. In our part of Russia, the Ukraine, there was no direct railroad going from north to south, or from east to west, and not all existing railroads connected with others. The Russian government was in the process of trying to complete its network of rails, but it would take time to do so. There were no timetables to give the schedule of any of them.

And so, we began walking the almost 275 miles south to Odessa, which is located on the Black Sea. One of my mother's sisters, my aunt Matya, lived there. There were many other refugees walking the roads, each headed toward friends or relatives who might be able to offer them food and shelter. Kolia walked some of the way, but mostly he had to be carried by Father or Mother. I can still remember seeing Kolia perched on my father's shoulders, looking about him like the king of all he surveyed!

When I felt I could go no farther without dropping from exhaustion, Father would say, "Come on, Tania. How about a piggy-back ride?" I would place my arms about his neck and hop up while he clasped his hands together behind his back, forming a basket-chair to help support my weight. Off he would trudge, my head resting on his shoulder, never complaining at the extra burden of my weight. How thankful I was at such times for my father's strength. Even as a child, I was aware of Father's deep love for each one of us, and of his willingness to sacrifice himself for us.

We did not stop too often during the day, but if we came to a little stream, we always stopped to refresh ourselves. We would splash water over our bodies, trying to cleanse away some of the soil of travel. Sometimes Mother would rinse articles of clothing in the running stream, and lay them out on the grass to dry. There were times when we even slipped the clothing back on while it was still wet, and allowed it to dry as we walked along.

At night we walked until we reached a village, and then Father would begin knocking on doors, introducing us as refugees from Kiev, on our way to Odessa, and asking if food could be spared for us, or shelter could be offered. Often he knocked on several doors before someone would give us food. The Russian people were always warmhearted, and if they refused to help us, it was because they were destitute themselves.

Sometimes we were offered food before Father even asked for it—a crust of bread or a bit of soup. We were always so grateful to receive it, because it was all we would have to eat until the next night's stop. Those nights we received nothing to eat, it was hard for me to go to sleep, knowing there would be a full day of walking the next day, and on an empty stomach. How we hoped for food at the end of the next day's journey!

Shelter was easier to find than food. The homes of these villagers were one-room huts, but most of them had a shanty-like structure in back, which was generally used for storage. We would be led out to this building, and invited to lie on the floor to sleep. The next day, we would continue our walking, grateful for the night's rest. We had no idea how long it would take us to reach our destination. At each village, my parents would ask, "Which way is it to Odessa?" "Is there a railroad around here?"

One day, we walked into a village with a railway station. There was no regular train service, now that Russia was at war, but if a train did happen to be making a run, and had any extra room aboard, refugees were allowed to ride free. It was so nice to be able to look out the window and realize we were not walking all those miles!

It took us about ten days to reach Aunt Matya's, and she welcomed us with tears and open arms. The Russian government had discontinued mail service. This meant that there was no way to contact loved ones to know whether they were safe. Here we were, terribly thin and unkempt, but safe. There were many questions to answer about what had been happening to our family since the fateful night of the attack on Kiev.

It was pleasant there on the Black Sea, and since Aunt Matya had a small garden, we stayed several weeks. Father had hoped there might be some type of work for him in Odessa, but the war had brought hard times here, as well. When it was obvious Aunt Matya could no longer feed four extra mouths, we knew we must head elsewhere. The decision was to head for Rovno, near which Mother had a brother and a sister. After tearful goodbyes—we didn't know if we would ever see one another again—we began the long trip north and west to Rovno, almost 325 miles from Odessa (200 miles west of Kiev).

Rovno! It was even farther away than Kiev! Would we ever reach it? I wondered if we would have to walk all the way. Any railroads in the direction we were traveling would undoubtedly have been taken over by the Germans. Russians are used to walking. We would walk! I knew that when I became too tired, there would be a piggy-back ride to give me a chance to regain my strength.

Again each night, Father was able to find shelter for us in the villages. One night when a woman opened the door, the delicious aroma of freshly baked goods wafted out. As I took a deep breath, my longing must have registered on my face. Before taking us out to our sleeping place, the woman went back into the room, got two of those precious warm pasties, about the size of hot dog buns, and handed them to Father. I will never forget how good they tasted. Even now, as I think of how little these people possessed materially, and how willing they were to share with refugee strangers, it brings tears to my eyes.

On occasion, someone would offer us a ride in a horse-drawn wagon. This was a welcome treat. My parents were always full of questions: "Are there German soldiers in this area?" "What news do you have of the war?" "Are the Russian soldiers returning to Kiev?" "Do you know how much farther it is to Rovno?" "Is it safe to go there?" Sometimes there was information, sometimes not.

As we drew closer to Rovno, we began to see German soldiers. Most walked, as we did; however, there were also military trucks and jeeps traveling the roads, and we gave all vehicles a wide berth.

There were many other refugees on the road, doing just as we were, hunting for food and shelter. It was becoming commonplace to see people lying by the side of the road, too weak from hunger to go any farther. Before we reached our destination, we would see thousands who had met death in this manner. Seeing them made us move more quickly, so death could not overtake us.

Patrolling soldiers began to stop us every few kilometers, to make sure we had no weapons. They would then ask where we were coming from, and where we were going. When they were satisfied that we were just another refugee family trying to survive the war, they would let us continue. Sometimes a patrol would ask us if we were happy to be under German rule. "Oh, yes," my father would smilingly answer.

I was so shocked the first time I heard Father give this answer that I could hardly wait until we were safely away from the patrol to exclaim, "Papa! How could you tell the soldiers we are happy they have invaded us?"

Father tenderly placed his arm about me as he explained. "Tania, the Bible tells us we are to be in subjection to those in authority over us. Right now the Germans are in authority. Our heavenly Father knows all about the situation, and that I must answer them in this way to ensure the safety of my family."

Our exact destination was Mikhaylovsky, a suburb north of Rovno. Mother's sister Paula and her brother, Ivan, both lived in this town. There was another tearful reunion when we all got together. How thankful we were to find that here were other members of our family who were safe.

Aunt Paula had a one-room hut, and we all slept together on the floor. Uncle Ivan had a larger house, with one bedroom, and an enclosed porch, where our family slept. We would spend two or three days at Aunt Paula's, then two or three days at Uncle Ivan's.

Father had a sister, Nastya, in the village of Tolokun, which was about a five-hour walk north of Mikhaylovsky. We walked up there to spend some time with her, and back to Mikhaylovsky.

When winter hit in full force, we had to have permanent shelter. More desperate than we had ever been before in our lives, we experienced a miracle. Father's brother Nikoly, whose house in Rovno had been taken over by the Soviets during the collectivization, was notified that it had been vacated in the Soviet retreat. Uncle Nikoly was now settled in Kiev. His two sons, loyal Communists, had access to food, and were supplying their father. Uncle Nikoly did not dare take advantage of this German offer to take his house back, for fear of being labeled an enemy sympathizer. His own sons would have persecuted him, and fearful reprisals would have come upon him when the Russians returned to power. So he sent word to let his brother Paul (my father) live there. Somehow the word got through to us, and for the first time in four months we had a place of our own in the town of Rovno. We hoped to stay there until the Russians returned.

The house was surrounded by a small apple orchard. Even though the branches of the trees had been destroyed by war, and by people seeking firewood, I remember

Father saying, "If only we can make it through the rest of the winter, we'll have some food of our own."

We struggled to keep warm. Every day we combed the woods for a fallen branch. We burned the rotting apple trees, one by one. It seemed a terrible, time-consuming job, leaving no time for anything else. We begged or earned just enough money for food to stay alive. At last we were reduced to eating grass when spring arrived. A dandelion became a special treat—when we happened to find one. We never let one blossom, but ate the leaves and stem as quickly as they appeared. Although it was a desperate time, the worst was yet to come.

During the winter, the Germans had been preoccupied with getting the city operating, taking a census of the people, and setting up areas of military jurisdiction. They had let the people settle down a bit into the occupation routine. With the spring of 1942 came the announcement that by May each family must choose one among them to serve in Germany for a three-month period in the war effort. Each person would be "well treated, given essential war work to do, and returned home at the end of that time, better off than before." That was the promise. A look at Father's face made me apprehensive. He said, "There is no question about it, I will go."

"No," said Mother, "I will go."

"But they want the young and the strong," I argued, "and Papa, what about Mama and Kolia? They need you. Mama, you are too weak. I must go."

My mother and father were silent. As torn as they were, they knew it was the only alternative. The day finally came, and the German Jeeps and trucks were lined up in the town square of Rovno. Since there was no railroad between Rovno and Kiev, we were to be transported by Jeeps and trucks to Kiev, where a rail line would make connections with other rail lines into Germany. Father would go with me on that ride to the city, but I would represent the family in the work conscription force. It seemed a hard decision for Father to make, but it was clear to me what we must do.

I hugged Mother and Kolia goodbye. Mother clung to me, and I thought, *Three months will not be too long, and then I will be back.*

My parents were saying their goodbyes. After riding to Kiev with me, Father would have to walk the hundred miles back to Rovno. In this time of war, personal safety was never guaranteed, and Father could only promise my mother that he would act with utmost care and be back at the earliest possible moment.

The Germans had told us everything would be provided for us, which was ironic, as I had nothing to take anyway. With just the clothes on my back, I walked slowly with Father to the waiting Jeep, treasuring every moment we had together. Our friends and neighbors all walked along beside us, bringing one family member to send away. They brushed past us, oblivious to everyone and everything but their own sorrow and loss, just as we were also oblivious to theirs.

The ride to Kiev went much too quickly. We were unloaded beside boxcars, their great, black mouths open to receive us. Father took off his hat and, with tears on his face, began to pray. I will never forget his words: "I give our beloved little Tania back to you, Lord. She is all yours again. Protect her, Father. Direct her steps. Spare her life. And please, God, let me meet her in heaven."

I was crying hard by this time. I had believed the German propaganda that I would be home with my parents again by summertime. My life in Russia up to that time had not been easy, so I believed nothing could be so bad that I couldn't stand it for that long. But suddenly I knew that my father didn't believe it. He was remembering the boastful threat of the Russians. The Communist Manifesto said, "Let the ruling classes tremble at a Communist revolution. The Proletarians have nothing to lose but their chains. They have a world to win." But here were the Nazis, ordering Communists at gunpoint to obey them. How soon the mighty had fallen! One could not trust in governments. One could not believe the promises of powerful men.

My father began searching through his pockets. "Tania, I wish I had something to give you—money, something." As he pulled out his wallet, he looked for a coin, but it was empty. Then, with a tender kiss, he handed me the empty wallet. "Keep this wallet, Tania; it's all I have to give you. Let it remind you of how much I love you." Today, that precious wallet—old, faded, its leather cracking—still reminds me of my father's love.

Father cupped my face in his hands and looked directly into my eyes. "I'll never see you again, Tatyana Pavlovna. Promise me and the Lord that you will meet me in heaven. There is nothing sure but that place. There is no hope but that hope. You've read God's Word, Tania. Promise!"

But I couldn't promise. It was such a serious decision, and I was so upset—so afraid. The weeping and moaning around me were punctuated with regularly barked German orders. How could I think? I did not know anything for sure. The last thing I wanted to do in this final moment among the anxious crowd was to lie to Father. But I could not think of such things. I would not believe his words. I would not think of the future because the present was so dreadfully at hand.

I was herded into a boxcar with others, packed in like an animal, with standing room only. I strained to see my father. Tears flooded my eyes as I hugged the wallet to me. Little did I know that his words were prophetic. Three months would stretch into eight years. I would never come home, and I would never see him again.

The door clanged shut, closing out even the dark skies over my beloved Kiev.

3

Early Years

And he went out, not knowing where he was going (Heb. 11:8).

Kiev, beautiful Kiev, was my birthplace and home for all but three years when I lived in Siberia. Kiev, located about 500 miles southwest of Moscow and 450 miles east of Warsaw, Poland, is the capital of the Ukrainian Soviet Socialist Republic. It stands tall on a high bank of the Dnepr River, and nestles between several hills opposite the mouth of the Desna River.

The Ukraine itself is in the extreme western part of Russia and has on its western border the countries of Poland, Czechoslovakia, Hungary, and Rumania. Wedged between the Ukraine and one section of Rumania is a tiny slice of land, the Moldavian S.S.R. The Ukraine's southern outlet is the Black Sea.

The Ukraine was annexed by Russia in 1924. Agriculturally rich, it presently supplies Soviet Russia with one-quarter of its grain.

Before I was born, the Stalin regime had begun the system known as "collectivization," at first on a voluntary basis. This system called for giving up individual owner-ship of lands, tools, and animals. The government then allotted an amount of land to each member farmer. A group of farms made up a "collective," and each collective was regarded as a cooperative. The government kept a record of all production from the collective, and each peasant farmer was remunerated with a share of that produce, in proportion to what was being produced.

However, under the voluntary system, not too many farmers were willing to join, especially in the Ukraine. Since some of the most vigorous resistance was being shown there, it was in the Ukraine that the Soviet government began concentrating its effort to force farmers to join. The year of my birth, 1929, an all-out effort was made to bring farmers into collectives.

Active resisters were labeled *kulaks*—"the rich ones." Their land and other property were confiscated by the government, and in many instances the resisters were deported to Siberia or central Asia. Passive resisters resisted in another manner. They cut back on the breeding of their animals, especially the horses, which were used for tilling the land. Other animals they slaughtered for food, rather than surrender them to the collective.

At that time my father was employed by the Russian government as a transportation engineer. He was skilled in planning and supervising the construction of much-needed rail lines. The ultimate goal of the government was to have a connecting rail network that would stretch from east to west, and from north to south.

At the same time collectivization was being enforced, the Russian government began also to encourage its citizens to populate the vast Siberian regions. In particular, they wanted families to locate in the Pacific coastal region. The fishing industry had created jobs in catching, processing, preserving, and shipping fish. Attractive salaries were promised to those who would relocate their entire families there.

My father opposed being a part of the collective. Feeling that his life could be no worse in Siberia than it was in the

Ukraine, he made plans to move. He also hoped that in the less-populated area he would be able to worship God with more freedom than he had in Kiev. Through my father's witness to him, his brother Dannis had recently become a Christian. Father persuaded Uncle Dannis that he should also leave Kiev and go to Siberia. He, his wife, and his two children joined our family about four months after we arrived.

My parents told us children the story of our life in Siberia many times as we were growing up in Kiev. It is from these stories that my memory of our family's sojourn in Siberia is formed.

When we left in 1930, there were only two children in our family—my four-year-old brother, Afanacy, and I, the baby, not yet a year old. My parents packed our few belongings and placed them in a horse-drawn wagon. When it was time to go, I was hiding under the bed, and Father finally had to use a stick to pull me out. Even then, I must not have wanted to leave the security of a known place. God began preparing me at an early age for the life I would have to endure later on.

We traveled in the wagon to the nearest railroad station having connections to the east. Of course, once on the train, it was not one long, uninterrupted trip. There were many places where we had to change trains or wait for a connecting train. Those days we literally lived in the depot. Father would go through the nearby neighborhood looking for work as a day laborer, while Mother stayed in the depot, caring for her two babies. Once we waited for two weeks for a connecting train. I cannot even imagine how my parents managed during that extended trip!

It took us three months to reach the Siberian Pacific coast. We traveled down the coast to a village called Rybolov, on a little lake called Ozero Khanka. We were not far from Vladivostok, which is a port city on the Sea of Japan—located to the northwest of Tokyo, Japan.

The government had promised jobs here, but had failed to say that each person would have to search for his own job. My father wasn't able to find work right away. New friends that he met at the fishery gave us a little one-room cabin to live in. It was the nicest place in which we ever lived. Although it was very small, it was in a rural area, and the uncrowded beauty of the stark countryside, the beautiful wooded area that surrounded us, the relative good health we were all enjoying, and, best of all, the freedom to move and speak and sing without fear of spies and reportings, brought real joy and contentment to our family.

There was a wooded area not more than a hundred feet from our cabin. Afanacy and I were cautioned not to go near it because of wild animals that were there. Once while I was playing near our log cabin, a huge black bear ambled out of the woods, reared to its full height, and stood there looking at me. When I saw it, I ran screaming to my mother. I certainly did not want to receive a hug from that bear!

Father finally found work with a fish packer, and brought home fresh fish during the fishing season. Fish were cheap, and we would preserve them by salting and hanging them up to dry on a long pole outside our cabin. No one ever stole anything from us there. To eat the fish, we would soak off the heavy salt coating in the lake or stream. In the winter, we would cut a hole in the ice to wash off the fish. Once Father took us to visit the packing plant, where we saw caviar, smoked fish, and canned fish stacked in what seemed mountainous piles.

Uncle Dannis and his family had arrived by this time, and there was real joy as the two brothers were able to worship God together, and to feel a new freedom in their Christian lives.

Father became the village lay pastor, and all the Christian families would gather at the largest of the houses to sing and share their faith. Then Father would bring a message from the Book that was so precious to him. We knelt to pray, and all the men and boys removed their hats out of respect to the great God we worshiped.

Singing was the one special enjoyment for old and young alike. After singing together for hours during our worship services, the grownups would sit around and talk, and the children would play. Here again, a favorite pastime was singing. After we tired of singing songs, we would cup our hands to our mouths, competing to see who could sing the highest tone. The one who sang the highest without breaking down in laughter was declared the winner amid many giggles.

In Rybolov, families shared more with each other of their faith than just words. When one family slaughtered a pig, all the others would receive a little piece of salt pork. My mother would measure off the piece with a knife to see how many days she could make it last for soup. Just a tiny piece would give the soup an interesting flavor. The growing season here was very short, and we had to buy potatoes and onions for our soup.

There were those Russians in our rural village fortunate enough to own a cow. So, in addition to fish, my father was able to buy milk for our family.

The method of storing milk during freezing weather presented an unusual sight. After milking time, the milk was left in the bucket to freeze, then knocked out and stored in huge chunks in cloth bags that hung beside the door of each house where a cow was owned. When there was an ample supply of frozen milk, it was taken by snow sled to Vladivostok where it was peddled. The money received would be exchanged for staple food supplies.

There were two new additions to our family while we

lived in Rybolov. Before I was three, Nadia was born—in 1931. About a year later, in 1932, Olga was born. The new baby sisters brought much happiness to our house. But just like so many other times in my life, happiness was not to last. Mother became very ill with the dreaded typhoid fever.

Father took her to the hospital in Vladivostok, and Uncle Dannis's family and other Christian believers, took care of us. It was a lonely time for Father and for us children. Mother was gone a long time, and we were overjoyed when she finally came home. We planned the future in our minds, with blind hope and the optimism born of youth. But then Mother had a relapse and was gone again for weeks. During the rest of our stay in Rybolov, she battled the disease cycle of recuperation and relapse, over and over again—hope rising; hope dashed.

The doctors advised my father to take us all home to Kiev, where the climate was more moderate and where several hospitals were available. It was with great sadness that we said goodbye to relatives and friends in Siberia, to begin the long journey back to Kiev. Uncle Dannis and his family remained in Rybolov. Ironically, my mother never did completely recover, and we went back to the worst of times for us as a family.

This was the winter of 1933, and Afanacy was now seven years old. I was four, Nadia was two, and Olga was one year old. If Mother's trip to the Pacific coast of Russia had been difficult, going back to Kiev, unwell, and with four children—three of them preschoolers—was to be even more difficult. Mother had to depend on Afanacy to help her care for the babies while Father was absent from us. There were the same delays in waiting for trains, the same number of times changing to other train lines, all in the dead of winter.

As difficult as things were, a terrible sorrow was to

overtake our family before we reached Kiev. If all had gone well, with no unexpected delays, we were due to reach Kiev within two weeks. On the way back, however, Nadia and Olga became ill, running high fevers. Then they broke out with German measles and were desperately ill. Since there was no doctor aboard the train, my father took us off at the first city we came to that was large enough to have a hospital. However, Father and the babies were refused admittance because of the communicable disease, and we were told that we must continue on to Kiev to seek medical help there. Helpless to do otherwise, Father placed us aboard the next train, and we continued our journey. My sisters' conditions continued to worsen, and both Father and Mother were literally exhausted from worry and from caring for Nadia and Olga day and night.

When we finally did reach Kiev, both of the babies were unconscious and had not responded for several hours. Police who were at the train station took them to the hospital for us, and my father took the rest of us to the apartment of our friends the Dmitrenkoses, where they had arranged to stay on arrival. Afanacy and I were beginning to run fevers, and my tired and weak mother had to care for us. When my father went to the hospital after getting us settled, he met with crushing news. Nadia had already died, and Olga died soon after he arrived.

Because of the communicable disease, the government officials took care of the burial for us. Father went alone to see them for the last time. He read the Bible and prayed in a little private funeral service. The rest of us grieved at home. By this time both Afanacy and I had come down with the measles. Mother was not able to leave us, and was too weak by this time to do anything other than care for us. I can remember how we cried to see the little ones. It was awhile before I realized I would never see them again.

4

Home Again

❋

Let us therefore come boldly to the throne of grace, that
we may obtain mercy and find grace to help in time of
need (Heb. 4:16).

When we arrived back in Kiev in the spring of 1933, we
found the Ukraine in an acute food shortage. While we
had been in Rybolov, an overwhelming majority of the
people throughout Russia had been absorbed into the
collective system. However, because of the passive resistance that had taken place in the Ukraine, the number of
work horses had been greatly diminished. Less horsepower meant less land tilled, which in turn meant less grain
grown and harvested. The Soviet government was producing tractors and combines as rapidly as possible, but they
were not able to produce an adequate amount quickly
enough to replace the lost horsepower.

As if this problem were not enough, a drought cut down
the grain production even further, and the Ukraine began
to experience a severe famine. The Soviet government
refused to admit the famine's existence and would allow
no disaster relief for the stricken areas. Those were the
conditions that met our family as we returned to Kiev to
make a new beginning.

When we moved in with the Dmitrenkoses, their son,
Vladimir, was eight, and their daughter, Maruska, was five.
Back in Mikhaylovsky, before my parents were married,

they had known this couple. Sharing their Christian faith with one another had drawn the four of them very close. Now we had arrived at their one-room apartment, penniless, ill, with nowhere to go. In love, they willingly took us in to share their shelter and food until we could get situated.

Father was able to find an abandoned hut—with a dirt floor and thatched roof. As soon as we were physically able to go, he moved us there. My parents were grateful to have this shelter free of charge.

Finding food became our first priority, especially since Father as yet had no job. When Afanacy and I were fully recovered from the measles, we became expert food hunters. We roamed about, looking for dandelion greens, or going from house to house, begging for vegetable peelings with which Mother could make soup. Sometimes we were even given dried sunflower or pumpkin seeds. They were delicious, and of good nutritional value. There was a special treat at Eastertime when we all attended the Greek Orthodox church to receive the eggs they gave to each child who attended the service. Birds were another source of food. Father showed Afanacy how to construct a *rogatka,* a type of slingshot. Before that desperate summer was over, both Father and Afanacy were expert hunters.

We had a tiny garden at this house, and we filled every inch of the space with seeds. There were carrots, onions, beets, cucumbers, a bit of leaf lettuce, five or six heads of cabbage, and even three potato vines—all that in an area about nine feet square! My mother had to watch Afanacy and me carefully. When something poked its head through the ground, we wanted to pull it up. Our stomachs swelled from malnutrition, but we managed to stay alive. When summer came and the garden matured, how thankful we were to have this fresh food to eat!

My mother's health did not permit her to do the hard labor that many Russian women were accustomed to doing—such as working with the Russian men on road construction.

Those mothers were not charged to bring their healthy children to government nurseries, but when children were ill, their mothers had to get someone to care for them at home. My mother made herself available to do part-time babysitting, though not much pay was involved. She also worked part-time for about three months at a bakery, helping to make the bread, and to clean the bakery kitchen afterwards. How we wished the bakery would pay her in bread, but of course that was not possible. The bakery had to account to the government for every loaf of bread they baked, and would not dare to give any of it away. She was able to bring home a small salary, instead.

It was fall before my father was rehired by the Soviet government, doing the same job as before he had left for Siberia. Once again he was employed as an engineer in the field of transportation, planning and supervising the construction of rail lines and roads in and near Kiev.

Since there were precious *rubles* being brought home, we were able to move from the abandoned hut in which we had been living to a one-room apartment owned by the government. Now we were neighbors with our friends the Dmitrenkoses, and my parents were happy to be living nearby another Christian family. This apartment not only had a wooden floor, but white-washed plaster walls and ceiling. With a blanket, my mother divided the room into two sections; one for sleeping, and the other for eating and living space.

The bed in our apartment was really a sleeping platform built of wooden boards. One board was permanently fastened to the wall, like a shelf, which became the head of the bed. Legs to support the platform were constructed, saw-horse-fashion, about eighteen to twenty inches high. Boards were laid, unfastened, outward from the shelf, at right angles from the head of the bed. This platform could be made wider as a family expanded. A new child in the family? Add another width of board. A quilt was laid over the sleeping platform to serve as a pad, and coats became our individual blankets. The whole family slept together on the platform—parents in the middle, children on either side of them. During the daytime, the boards were removed and stacked on the shelf-headboard, and the bed became a bench on which to sit.

Built into the opposite corner from the bed was a stove, called the *petch*. This structure, which somewhat resembled a raised open fireplace, was a very important part of any Russian home. It was our only means of cooking, and our only source of heat in the winter. Made entirely of bricks, it was square in shape, and built on a base that was wider and a little longer than the oven itself. Not every *petch* was the same size. The one in our apartment was almost six feet square. The base was about twenty-four inches high and hollow under the front of the oven, forming a large area that was used for storage. The actual opening of the oven was in the shape of a half-circle, with a work area in front, on top of the extended part of the base. The chimney rose directly up above the oven opening, leaving a good-sized area behind it that made a warm place to spend a cold evening, or to curl up on to sleep. In the wintertime, my mother spread the quilt on top of the *petch* and our whole family slept there. On cold winter nights we were glad for the warmth of the bricks underneath us.

The fire was made toward the back of the *petch*. My mother was tiny, and she was always glad to have my father start the wood fire for her, since he could reach farther back into the oven. There was never a problem with smoke, since it moved forward along the top of the oven and was drawn up through the chimney. When the embers were just right for cooking, my mother would use a long-handled fork to lift the cooking utensil by its curved rim and place it in the oven. We had a crockery pot to heat water for tea, and another crockery pot for soup. We had a cast-iron skillet that would be used to render fat from salt pork to use as flavoring for soup. In the fall, when vegetables had been harvested and were less expensive to buy, we could look forward to having a stew with some cabbage, a potato, a few carrots, an onion, and a bit of salt. How good it smelled cooking! On special occasions such as Easter or Christmas, if we had enough potatoes, my mother boiled them and added a pinch of dill.

We each had a spoon and fork, but there were only two cups. We ate from a common bowl placed in the center of the table. This was a beautiful wooden bowl, about nine inches in diameter, and six inches deep, with flowers painted around the outside.

Outside the apartment building was the pump where we got our water supply, and where my mother washed our clothes. My mother filled a tub with water, and using a bar of brown soap, scrubbed the clothes by hand. After all the white things had been scrubbed, Mother rubbed soap on them, put them in the heavy tub, and added enough water to cover them. Father would lift the heavy container and place it over a fire contained in a brick hearth. The clothes were boiled to sterilize them, and allowed to remain overnight. The next day when they were rinsed and laid out to dry, they would be snowy white. When I was older, I helped Mother with these jobs.

My family did not own a spinning wheel or a loom, but those families who did shared their treasures. Spinning and weaving were usually done during the winter. When my mother was able to have a turn, she knew just how to spin the thread, to be woven later on a loom for linen towels, or a woolen blanket. We had one large square pillow, handmade, filled with chicken feathers, and covered with linen.

My mother made all our clothing, including underwear and coats, by hand. My dress was long, and made of flannel; in the winter, when temperatures dipped below zero, and I was walking to school, I was glad for these warm things. All of my undergarments were made of flannel or unbleached muslin. These were made from purchased fabric, rather than fabric crafted by hand. For only a short time in any given period in my life did my clothes fit me. For a long time they were too large, and then they were too small. I remember crying for a new coat once, because mine was so threadbare. My mother carefully took the coat apart, turned the fabric inside out, and sewed it together again. One garment lasted a long time that way, but I longed for something new, different, and comfortable. As garments became threadbare, Mother neatly patched them. Shoulder and elbow areas received many patches, as did the seat area of Father's and Afanacy's trousers. Father had a suit that was purchased, but it was only worn on special occasions.

Shoes had to be purchased. Mine always started out too large, so they would last as long as possible. In the winter, we wore leather boots lined with felt, much like the snowmobile boots of today.

Once a week, the laundry tub was brought inside the house so that we could bathe. Mother heated water in the crockery pots for this purpose, and shampooed and rinsed my hair. Next she added more water to the tub, and in I went. When I was small, there was room to sit comfortably. As I grew older and larger, it became necessary to squat in the tub. After my bath came Afanacy's turn to bathe—in the same water. Sometimes he got the first turn. Of course, we each wanted to be first, to have the benefit of the clean water.

The toilet, which served all the families in the apartment, was in a separate building. Toilet paper was a newspaper or magazine, and each family took its turn furnishing it. First, the newspaper or magazine was passed around until it had been read by everyone who wanted to, and then it was placed on a nail in the outhouse for all to use. I can remember our family being given newspapers so wrinkled that they could not easily be read. Then Mother would put her iron inside the *petch* to heat it—just to a warm temperature—and smooth out the newspaper by ironing it carefully.

I never read those magazines or newspapers. Those jumbled characters meant nothing to me.

"Just think, Tania," my parents would say, "one of these days you will also be able to read these words."

They were preparing me for the completely new experience in store for me—for looming on my young horizon was the magic place called *school.*

5

A Child in Kiev

✳

Children, obey your parents in the Lord, for this is right (Eph. 6:1).

School started for me when I was five. Because there was no kindergarten in Russia, students began their studies at the age of five, and attended school six days a week for ten years. After graduation, they took examinations to see if they qualified to continue their education in the university.

We stood when the teacher entered the room, and said, "Good morning;" we stood when the teacher left the room, and said, "Good evening;" and we stood when the teacher addressed us by name and answered, "Yes, Sir," or "Yes, Ma'am."

Early games that we played were many of the same ones played by children in the United States. We played hide-and-seek, hopscotch, and marbles, too, when we could find smooth stones. We didn't have a real jump rope, but a piece of rope from Aunt Paula's farm served as well. Mother taught me to make a doll from a rag stuffed with scrap paper, to tie off head, arms, and legs, and to draw a face with charcoal. Imagination did the rest.

We had a regular time to be home from school, and our parents were very strict about it. One day however, I did not make it home on time. The Desna River ran parallel to the road I took home, and it was frozen over. I decided to go sliding—it was great fun to slide in my big boots, and the time passed swiftly. Suddenly I fell through the ice—coat, boots, books, and cloth lunch bag. Someone had cut a hole in the ice to rinse their clothes, and I had not seen the slushy spot in time. There was no one with me at the time, and I began desperately to grab the edge of the ice and crawl up. Each time though, the ice broke off in my hands. Thoroughly chilled and exhausted, and just when I thought I would never make it, I was able to grasp a piece of ice that held, and inch my way out onto a solid surface.

I lay there a full minute, resting and sobbing tears of thankfulness to be out of that icy water. It was getting dark by this time. Shaking from the cold, and with chattering teeth, I knocked on the door of the closest hut. What a sight I must have been—a little bedraggled girl, already beginning to be covered with icicles. Without a word they pulled me inside, quickly undressed me, and wrapped me in a blanket and placed me over the warm *petch* to recover from my icy ordeal.

One of them hurried off to tell my parents what had happened. My parents had been frantic with worry, and rushed back to bring me home. After greeting me with tears of relief, they alternately scolded and hugged me all the way home. "Don't ever do that again!" they said over and over—as if I had wanted to do it in the first place! In between their scolding and hugging, I wondered how I had ever gotten out of the water. Was there some reason that my life had been spared?

I was to have another brush with death, about a year later when I was six. Father and I were going across the Dnepr River to town. As we waited for the ferry boat, it began to rain. There was an overturned canoe lying on the bank, and we crawled under it for shelter. Soon someone tugged at Father's leg. Father thought it was someone wanting to share our shelter, but when he looked out, he saw the familiar face of the Russian soldier who, years before, had told my father about his own personal relationship to the Lord Jesus. He had asked Father if he would like to place his faith and trust in that same Lord Jesus, and was able to rejoice as he saw Father born into God's family.

After all these years, they were meeting under a canoe during a rainstorm to renew their friendship. The soldier was passing through Kiev on an assignment, and had reached the river bank at the same time we had. When he asked someone to direct him to our home, that "someone" happened to be one of our neighbors, who had seen Father and me crawl under the canoe. What a reunion they had, hugging and kissing while praising God for his goodness in allowing them to see one another again. Since the soldier was on assignment, he was not able to come back to our home to visit for a longer time, but had to continue about his government assignment. Father assured me later that this meeting was not just a coincidence, but that God had arranged the meeting.

After Father's friend left us, the ferry came and we boarded it. The Dnepr was wide and deep in this part of the city, and the ferry boat was the best means to get from one section of the city to another. The bridge, which was not close by, was mainly used by vehicle traffic, and was dangerous for pedestrians.

The rainstorm had intensified, and the wind had risen, blowing in strong gusts, making the ferry's progress difficult. It was loaded with people, all of us trying to shelter ourselves from the storm. Suddenly a gust of wind rocked the boat to one side, causing people to tumble and fall in the direction the ferry was leaning, and the weight shift caused the ferry to swamp. Father grabbed me and jumped clear of the capsizing boat, into the water. Sailors quickly cast off the rubber life rafts, and Father lifted me into one, crawling in after me. He helped others into the boat, and then paddled for shore. Again that day, Father said to me, "This was not by chance, Tania, that our lives were spared. This is another thing that God has arranged."

The summer that I turned seven, 1936, we made walking trips to see Aunt Paula at Mikhaylovsky. We always went to see Mother's brother, my uncle Ivan, while we were at Mikhaylovsky, but we spent most of the time at Aunt Paula's. Mother's ties were closer to her sister than to her brother.

That was the first complete summer I remember spending with Aunt Paula. Since my mother was now working, she decided it would be less lonely for me to be with Aunt Paula for the summer. Then too, Aunt Paula needed someone to help her with her garden, cow, pigs, and chickens. As small as it was, the Soviets called it a farm, and it was registered as part of a collective. Careful records were made by government officials of how much milk the cow gave, how many eggs the chickens laid, and how well and how much the garden was producing. These records, of course, would be the means of determining the share Aunt Paula would return to the government. Present records were constantly being compared with the previous ones, to make sure no collective member could manage to keep a few extra eggs or a quart of milk for himself.

Aunt Paula taught me to recognize the difference between a weed to be pulled and a vegetable to be left in the ground. She taught me to feed the animals. I loved to hear the pigs squeal as they rooted for their food. I loved to throw the feed out to the chickens, and watch their heads clustered together, bobbing up and down, with tails high in the air as they noisily fought to get their share of food— and hopefully someone else's too!

The fresh vegetables and milk and occasional meat that I received at Aunt Paula's were welcome experiences for me. No wonder I looked forward to spending summers there.

My parents and Afanacy always walked over to Aunt Paula's sometime during the summer, to see how I was getting along. Then at the end of the summer, they came again to take me back home. Aunt Paula would load us down with a precious burden: a portion of meat, beet greens, carrots, and onions. We knew this would be made into a delicious stew when we reached home. What a special treat to look forward to!

As we walked along, Afanacy and I would beg Father: "Tell us about when we were little, and lived in Siberia." Another time we might ask, "How did you and Mother meet?" Of course, we had heard those stories many times, but we never tired of hearing them again. Father would quickly glance at Mother, and with a twinkle in his eyes, would ask her, "How about it; do you want to hear *that* story again?" Mother would always give him a tender smile as her answer. We would walk along together, the four of us, engrossed in the story we knew so well.

"I was born Paul Awdienko, in the little village of Tolokun, as you know. Aunt Nastya is the only one of my family who still lives there. We left Uncle Dannis in Rybolov, Siberia, and Uncle Nikoly lives in Kiev. As a young man, I was in the Russian army and played the clarinet in the army band. There I met another musician who was a Christian. I could tell he was different. You met him, Tania; remember the day we took cover under the canoe during the rainstorm? He is the one who told me that God loved the world so much that He sent His Son here to this earth, to die on the cross, to pay the penalty for our sins. How I thank God that my friend kept telling me, until I was willing to put my faith and trust in the Lord Jesus Christ.

"In the meantime, there was a young lady, Hrunia Werba, whose name means 'puny willow tree.' You can see how tiny she is, and how her name really suits her. She was born in Mikhaylovsky, along with your Aunt Paula, Aunt Matya, and Uncle Ivan. Her parents were farmers, just as mine were. Aunt Matya lives down in Odessa, which is located on the Black Sea.

"While your mother was very young, she married a Soviet sailor who was a friend of mine and bore him a son. Then a double tragedy struck. Her husband's ship sank at sea, with no survivors, and then her baby died in infancy. She was visiting at her husband's parents' home, recovering from these blows. When I returned, discharged from the Russian army, I went to their home, only to discover that my friend had died. At the same time, I met his young widow. I was attracted to her, and spent a lot of time at the home where she was staying. We had one thing in common; we both loved music.

"I wanted us to have one more thing in common. I began talking to her about the Lord Jesus, as my friend had talked to me. When I asked her to accept the death of Jesus Christ on the cross as the penalty paid in full for her sins, she did just that, and she was born that day into God's family.

"After this, I courted her in earnest. I knew that I loved her, and wanted to spend the remainder of my life with her. When I asked her to marry me, I found that she felt the same way, and she told me that she would marry me. After we were married, first you were born to us, Afanacy; and three years later, you were born, Tania. When you were four and one, we went to Rybolov, clear across Russia, to the Sea of Japan. There is where your sisters Nadia, and later Olga were born."

Here my father's arm would find its way around my mother's shoulder, as they remembered their double sorrow at losing the two babies to the German measles.

Then with the end of the story, he would sometimes

break out into song, in his rich baritone that we loved to hear. We would join him in singing as we walked along. Or perhaps he would point out birds to us, and we would listen to their song. As we neared Kiev, we would step up our pace, anxious to get back to our little home. Another summer was over, and it was time for school to begin again.

6

Growing Up Years

✳

We are hard pressed on every side, yet not crushed; we are
perplexed, but not in despair; persecuted, but not forsaken;
struck down, but not destroyed. (2 Cor. 4:8–9).

In the seven years that I attended school in Russia, I
remember having classes in reading, spelling, mathematics,
writing, history, science, geography, and shorthand.

One day in a spelling class, I remember our teacher's
having an attack of some sort. (I believe now that it must
have been an epileptic seizure.) He was showing the class
an especially good paper of mine when he fell on the floor
beside me. I was so frightened that I jumped right through
the casement window of the room, and ran (with all the
class following me) to the front door where we told our
problem to the headmaster.

One important required subject for every Russian child
was a study of Marxist doctrine. In that class I learned that
Russia is the largest, most powerful, and best nation in the
world. "We don't need anyone else," they taught me. I
learned that I must not trust teachers, neighbors, or friends.
Any one of them might be a spy. All of us were taught
loyalty to the state, and the necessity of reporting to the
authorities such a family as mine, who sang songs of God
in their home, and who had a copy of the Bible in their
possession. Here I learned that my family was a dangerous
one. I learned to be secretive, and to tolerate fear. I

suffered emotionally and physically, but grew stronger through that suffering. This school prepared me for a life I would never have chosen for myself, but one that was to be mine, nevertheless.

Every room in the school had a wood stove, and it was necessary for someone to be responsible for the fire each day during cold weather. Someone had to clean around the stove, cut and supply wood, and lay and light the fire early in the morning, before school started. As I grew older, I remember taking this job often. For doing this, I received a free lunch at school, and a very small allowance. It helped keep me from starving, and gave my family a little extra money. I look back and see how much of my life was food-oriented. My stomach never lets me forget!

One of our after-school activities was hunting vegetables in the government fields. After harvest, the fields were fair game for anyone. As a group we would make our plans at recess to look for food. We made it into a game, searching each hill from which the potatoes had been dug, and squealing with delight when we found even one small, precious vegetable. What thrill and excitement there were when we found a whole hill that had not been overturned!

We searched the beet and onion fields, sometimes taking an extra slice of bread and some salt from home (imagine stealing from your own family). When we found an onion, we would bite it into chunks, put it on the bread, sprinkle the salt on it, and sit down to a feast before we went home. Can you imagine what our breath smelled like afterwards?

We combed the grass for mushrooms, and even picked up grain that had fallen in the wheat fields. It had to be carefully sifted and cleaned by straining it through a cloth when we got it home, but it could be ground into flour and baked into precious bread.

The whole family rejoiced and gave us hugs and kisses for each find. We drew closer because we were so dependent upon each other—parents upon children, and children upon parents. There was very little child delinquency in that day.

We preserved our food by drying it. When the apple harvest came in, we bought a bushel and ate only the bruised ones. The rest we cut and dried in small pieces to be made into sauce later on, or to use to flavor our tea in the winter. When the deep snow of winter came and kept us from our hunting, we existed on dried food and bread until spring.

Our evenings at home were very special to us. My tall, blond, handsome father sang to us each night in his rich baritone. First, the Holy Scriptures, put to beautiful melodies, would fill the room. Then came songs recalling the days when he was a soldier and played the clarinet in the Russian army band. Some songs were of friendship, like the friendship he shared with the bandsman who led him to know God through Jesus Christ. But some songs were love songs, and we followed his smiling eyes across the table to where Mother sat quietly listening or joining in with her sweet soprano.

Father carried his little Bible everywhere, hidden in his clothes, even when discovery could have meant prison. That book seemed to be his most precious possession. It must have given him extra strength. How else could he work for two weeks for 250 *rubles,* only to spend 175 of them for a pound of sugar, or a pair of shoes? How else could he bear the haunting injustice of the confiscation of his family's property to the collective? How could a man sacrifice, day after day, for others with no seeming thought for himself?

He set an example for the family as well as faithfully providing for them. I remember his saying so often, "How I wish I could give you more," and I now know how much he gave. Often he did not eat, so that we children might have more. He took the heavy part of all the work, and worked at it longer than all the rest of us.

There were times he was called in to be questioned by the government authorities, who carefully watched their employees. "Why don't you drink with the other men? Why don't you laugh at their jokes? Why don't you swear?" My father would answer them humbly, "That's just the way I am."

However, if opportunity presented itself among those men he worked with, he witnessed of the God who sustained him, the Christ who saved him, and the Holy Spirit who indwelt him. I was not like him. I did not strongly believe in God, nor did I tell others about God.

My mother was tiny, and not a strong woman, especially after her extended illness in Rybolov. She did what she was able to do. Along with baby-sitting, she sometimes tackled harder jobs, such as white-washing a neighbor's house for an extra loaf of bread for her family. She mixed chalk and water, and gathered long dried grass to bind into a brush to cover the inside and outside of the house with the paint substitute. The method was primitive, but clean and cheap. Sometimes she gathered more of the long dried grasses, tied them in bundles, and sold them to people for fuel. Her goal was always enough money to buy another loaf of bread.

My mother had few friends besides our neighbors the Dmitrenkoses, but they were all Christians. In spite of the many tragedies in her life—ill health, family deaths, and daily drudgery amidst starving living conditions—she was filled with praise to God, and would break out in hymns of joy regularly during the day. Loyal Soviets would have to report such Christian activity, and so she kept to herself, sharing her faith only with other Christians.

She faithfully cared for her home and family. They were her life. She taught me more by what she was than by what she said. Always patient and gentle and kind, I learned a little of what God's love is like from her faithful, sacrificial love for me. I was so unlike her—impatient, independent, and loud. Sometimes I wondered, if women were supposed to be like Mother, why was I not born a man?

Something exciting happened in our family in 1938, when I was in the fifth grade. My darling brother Nikoly was born. Most babies in Russia were delivered at home with the assistance of a midwife, but I knew, from listening to her talk with the other women, that something was wrong with Mother, though I didn't quite understand what it was.

One morning, I woke up to find Maruska's mother in our house, and she told me my mother was in the hospital. When she came home in a couple of days, she brought a baby boy with her. I couldn't figure it out. Mother had gone to the hospital before, but never brought a baby home. "Where did he come from?" I asked. "Who gave him to us?"

Mother just smiled, and answered, "He is God's gift!"

I could believe that, because he was blond and beautiful and perfectly formed. Oh, how I loved him, and eagerly watched as Mother nursed him until he could eat potato soup. I took care of him for my mother while she worked, on days when I did not go to school, or when he was not in the government nursery.

One day, when I was supposed to be watching him, I wandered away with my friends while he was sleeping. We found an old boat and oars in a nearby stream, and let our imaginations run wild. Time passed quickly, until suddenly with a shock, I remembered Nikoly. I ran home screaming, "My brother, my brother!" His face was red and swollen from crying and rubbing his eyes with his tiny fists. Even though my parents were not home, I knew I would have to tell them. They expected complete honesty from me, and I loved and respected them too much to disobey. When my parents returned, and I told them what had happened, each of them spanked me. My father had me cut my own switch, and after he used it on me, he put it up on two nails on the wall, to remind me each time I saw it. Then he took me on his lap, and hugged me, and said, "Do you know why I did that, Tania? Because I love you!" I never doubted that he did, and I clung to him, sobbing out my repentance. I never left my brother alone again.

There was a special reason why it was important to my parents that we children obey them. The government looked for opportunities to take children away from parents whose loyalty to the state was questionable, or for small things like truancy or tardiness in school. They were put in government correction homes, never to see their parents again, and the state gained loyal Communists. My parents trained us with love and that switch to get to school, to do our work, and to come straight home, unless we had their permission to look for food.

The happiest days of the month were Father's two paydays. On these days men and women would line up at the bakeries or food stores to buy a two-week supply of bread and staples. You had to keep your place in line, or others would buy up all the food, and you wouldn't get any. Wives would stand in their husbands' places, taking turns keeping their spot of power to purchase. As I got older, I would take my turn standing in the food line to relieve my parents. When I got close to the head of the line, it seemed my stomach hurt more and more. Sometimes it happened that I was at the head of the line for the family when it reached the store, and could actually be the one to purchase the bread.

Even then, we were never sure that it would be a full loaf that we could purchase. Those who were selling would look at the length of the line, and gauge how much they should sell to each person, to make it go as far as possible. Sometimes they cut the loaf in half, and sold it that way. If the line was especially long, they might even cut it into thirds. I would carry the bread home carefully, hoping I could last until I reached our apartment. But often I couldn't, especially when it was just a partial loaf. Then I would eat it all, with no thought of the hungry family at home.

You might say, "That's a child for you," but in reality, that is what starvation had done to me. You might think my parents would scold me, but although his eyes were sad, Father would say, "Tania, I'm glad you did that. You are growing, and you needed that food. I'm sorry that I can't provide enough for you so you wouldn't be so hungry." The kindness of my father only made me feel worse.

When I would win the battle against hunger and get the bread home, we would gather around the table and spread slices of bread with lard, a special treat, or dip it in the soup Mother would have made with potatoes, salt, and water. The rest we would lay out in the sun, or dry it in the petch to preserve it. This hard toast was indeed our "daily bread."

I always looked forward to spending the summer with Aunt Paula for this reason, even though it meant spending the whole summer away from my baby brother. We seldom called him Nikoly, but instead by the pet name, Kolia.

The summer at Aunt Paula's after Kolia was born, I got a job. First, I became a cowherd. Many people had only one cow. Each person who had one took turns watching it, and those of their neighbors, in the pasture. For a little food to take home to my family, I would watch up to forty cows in a herd, driving them out to pasture in the morning, and bringing them back to their owners' homes in the evening. I had a whip and felt important; but I seldom used it. The cows became my friends. Each one had a name, which, translated into English, would be *Spot, Silky, Blacky,* or *Whitey.* I learned to control them by talking to them, and that satisfied my loneliness too. All the cows were registered with the government—as were the chickens—for the milk and eggs belonged to the state. Only a small portion was left to the owner for his reward in caring for them for the people's republic.

When my parents, with Afanacy and Kolia, came to bring me home at the end of the summer, my parents began pointing out landmarks: "Do you remember that house, Tania? Look...when you reach this point where the road angles off, that tree over there will point the direction to go. Now remember that, so you will know the route for yourself, without getting lost." I didn't realize at the time their reason for teaching me the route.

School began all too soon, it seemed. My parents emphasized again the need for us to be home immediately after school. There were too many children who had disappeared during school hours, or just afterward. No trace of them would be found. And strangely enough they were usually members of the "troublesome" families, like Christian ones.

One day it was my brother Afanacy who did not return home from school on time. As it became late, my parents were frantic. "Tania, did you see your brother after school?" It so happened that I had; some men were talking to him, but I did not realize that anything was amiss. My parents immediately knew what had happened. They wept and prayed, and hugged Kolia and me.

Father reported to the police that Afanacy had disappeared, but though they promised to investigate, Father never could get any information when he went to the station. He believed it was a threat, because we were Christians. He knew Afanacy would never have run away. Afanacy loved his home. The bond between him and my parents was special.

You see, Afanacy was different. He listened to Father's words about the Christian message, and he believed what Father taught him about God. He didn't do the things the other children did. He was loving, and never pinched or beat up younger children as others his age did. He wouldn't "tattle" on others to the teacher, or report suspicious actions to the government. Because he was different, he was often alone. As I look back now, perhaps he was feared; perhaps that is why he was taken away.

Once after Father had been to the police station to inquire for information about Afanacy, and was returning home frustrated again, he stopped and bought me a piece of hard candy—one of the two times in my childhood that I tasted it. He took me on his lap and told me we would never see Afanacy again, and we never did. The candy comforted me as I cried for my thirteen-year-old brother.

That same summer of 1939, when I was almost ten, I discovered the reason my parents wanted me to learn the landmarks of the route to Aunt Paula's. Maruska, who was eleven, and I set off for Mikhaylovsky by ourselves. "Now, remember the landmarks you were taught, so you won't get lost. And when you ask to sleep at a house, remember how to be polite and courteous."

Off we went, filled with a new sense of adventure. Maruska had both friends and relatives not too far from where Aunt Paula lived. Her parents would be coming for her at the end of the summer, as would mine for me. And I knew my family would be coming for a midsummer visit, to make sure all was well with me.

Maruska and I seldom walked on the main road, but on

the footpaths on each side of it. Maruska on one, I, on the other. We would run along together, arms churning back and forth, heads bent, but stealing a look at each other on occasion.

When we finally felt the need to stop and rest, we would walk along, picking the wild flowers that were in bloom, and braiding them together as we walked, making ourselves a lovely flower headpiece to wear. We became grand ladies with lovely fragrant crowns! Then beginning to giggle uncontrollably, we would set off at a run again.

As we joined each other to walk side by side on the road, I would begin to make up songs. I would sing one for Maruska.

> A crying beautiful bird,
> In pain from a broken wing.
> He cannot fly now,
> Or even sing.
> But the Lord Jesus knows his need,
> And makes him well again.
>
> Now the beautiful bird says,
> "Thank You, my Maker,
> For what You did for me.
> Now I can fly again,
> And sing again for Thee."

"How did you make up that song, Tania?"

"I don't know."

"Where did it come from?"

"Just out of my head. I don't know."

"Sing it again!" And I would sing it until Maruska had learned it, and then we sang it together. As I would think of the things my father had taught me about God, I would make up another song:

The way to salvation
Is only through Christ,
And through His work
Which is open to us.

If we only are willing
To believe and receive
That He bought us with His life
At the cross of Calvary.

"I like that one too, Tania. Teach that one to me." And we would continue walking and singing.

That afternoon Maruska asked, "Do you suppose we'll have a problem asking for a place to sleep tonight?" That had been bothering me, too. My father always knocked at a door with confidence, and was so pleasant, people always seemed glad to accommodate us.

We could see a couple of people in the distance behind us, and we slowed down to allow them to overtake us.

"Hello, girls; how are you today?"

"Just fine, thank you."

We were glad, as evening was approaching, not to be alone. Perhaps this couple lived near here, and we might sleep at their hut. We would watch where they went.

Sure enough, they turned in at a hut, but they knocked. Oh! They wanted to stay the night themselves! We stood a little behind them, and as we heard the people who owned the hut say, "Yes, you may sleep inside here on the floor," we slipped in behind them, without saying a word, and lay down on the floor beside them. The next morning we were up and gone before anyone else awoke. How we giggled when we thought of what we had done—slept the whole night alongside people who were perfect strangers to us.

Maruska and I had always been "best friends," but this two-day walk brought us even closer together. We hated to part when we reached Aunt Paula's. We gave each other a hug, promising to see each other again in Kiev when it was time for school to begin.

That summer, as well as helping Aunt Paula with the garden chores, I again herded cows. The owners alternated preparing a lunch for me to eat at noon. At the end of the summer, they contributed a bit of food to send home with my family.

The summer of 1940, when I was almost eleven, I got a new job, as a recordkeeper for the government. I checked the milk that the farmers turned over to the state. Since I was good at mathematics, and was not a resident of Mikhaylovsky, I got the job. Apparently the government officials felt they could depend on a nonresident to keep accurate records. I had the record book with each family's name and each piece of livestock registered to them listed on a separate page. In the book was the total milk-giving record of the animal for preceding years. As the farmers brought in their milk to the receiving station, I would weigh it and record it after their name, and then multiply the liters by a few *kopecks* to see what the state would reimburse the farmer. Even though it was pitifully little, I didn't dare lie.

While I was out in the pasture, I learned to find wild berries of various kinds—blackberries, blueberries, and raspberries. Surprisingly, I remember them as larger than the wild ones I find near my home now. Perhaps it seems that way to me because they were such a treat. Aunt Paula was always glad when I brought berries to her, and she made a special Russian fruit dumpling. If I found enough, and she had sugar saved up, she made a little jam. Usually a small container of it went home with us at the end of the summer, for a once-a-year treat for our family. Oh, how good that tasted on our hard, dry bread! Because being desperately hungry was very vivid to me, food was always on my mind. I look back on those summers spent with

Aunt Paula as some of the most pleasant times of my childhood. Little did I know, though, that that would be my last summer at Aunt Paula's.

Later, as I traveled in the boxcar toward Germany, all these memories, both good and bad, would occupy my thoughts.

7

Inside the Boxcar

✳

For strangers have risen up against me,
And oppressors have sought after my life (Ps. 54:3).

As our train bound for Germany steadily took me farther away from my family, I cried in the darkness of the boxcar. But soon I became aware of a quietness around me. Everyone seemed to be resigned to his fate, and tears last only so long.

We were packed in too tightly to fall over with the lurch and sway of the train, and there was no room to sit down. This was all right for the first night, and mercifully we didn't know that that night would stretch into three weeks before we reached our destination.

From time to time I would doze off, only to awaken at a sudden extra lurch of the train, surprised that I had been sleeping. As morning arrived, I began looking about me, noticing things I hadn't been able to see in the darkness. The only light and air came from two small screened openings, high on the outside walls, and about twenty by nine inches in size. I continued looking, wondering how many of us were in the car—50, 100, 500—I didn't know, and I couldn't count them all, though at times I tried, for want of something to do.

Four German soldiers stood guard in our boxcar—two stationed on one side in front of a door, and two on the other side in front of the other door. One or even two of the soldiers might be sleeping, but the others were alert, with submachine guns ready to be used if necessary.

The train stopped once a day to allow the prisoners to relieve themselves and get water. We never knew when to expect the train to stop, but we were thankful when it did. We could get off the train and stretch and get a precious drink. The water that the train carried in tank cars was warm and tasteless, but we almost died for it, and fought for a place in line to get it. Each boxcar was opened separately, one door or the other—we never knew ahead of time which door would be opened. As soon as the door of our car rolled grindingly open on its rusty bearings, we would fall over each other getting out, and would run into the field to try to find a bit of privacy. Usually there was none. While at first it was embarrassing, toward the end of the forced journey, it was no longer of any concern. All the while the guards stood at trackside with submachine guns sighted on us. When they barked an order, we came quickly back to the train to try to get a drink. We had to hurry, and within a very short time we were all herded back into our rectangular steel prison, and the door clanged shut.

Sometimes we would stop for no apparent reason. Then we would hear planes overhead, and realize the Germans had stopped, hoping the enemy pilots would believe it to be an abandoned train. A moving train, of course, would mean that supplies or munitions were being moved, and would be a target. Sometimes it was a short delay, but there were times we would remain stopped for several hours. We would take advantage of this time to sleep, if we could, without the movement and "clackety-clack" of wheel upon rail. During these stops I learned to appreciate just the peace and quiet of no movement.

I also found that these were the only times I could talk to

anyone other than the persons on either side of me. On one of the first relief stops, I discovered a young girl, Jennie, just a few years older than I, who was from Kiev. We managed to get back into the car together each time so we could be near each other. We talked and whispered to each other all the time, and became the best of friends. An older woman from a village near Kiev also became our friend, and what a friend she was! She kept us alive by sharing her food with us.

Because we had had so little food at home, and because I never had dreamed that the Germans would not feed us, I hadn't taken any food with me. After the third day my stomach began to hurt terribly. Others in our car had wisely stuffed dried bread into their clothing. When I cried with hunger, this woman friend shared a crust with me.

We lived daily in hope of arriving at our destination. When it didn't happen, we had to organize. The older members of the crowd took stock of what food we had corporately, and rationed it out mouthful by mouthful. In all those three weeks on the train, the Germans never gave us a bite of food to eat. I guess I should be thankful that they gave us water.

We began to get weak. Since we were packed in so tightly, we leaned against each other. At the beginning we cared about each other, but as time wore on, our bodies ached, our stomachs hurt, our brains became numb, and we began to think only of ourselves. When someone fell into unconsciousness and slipped to the floor, we didn't feel a thing. We stood right on those fallen bodies, and wept only for ourselves.

The worst part of it all was the smell. The window openings were so small that not much fresh air could get to us. People became sick and vomited on themselves and others in the car. Perspiration made our clothes stick to us. Diarrhea added its own nauseating odor, as did the dried blood of menstruation. Most people could have stood the hunger, but the intensified odor made everyone ill. I was nauseated constantly for days, and I cannot count the hours I spent retching. I was sure I would die before I got anywhere, and I wondered how my father's prophecy could come true so soon. I wished I could have died back in Russia, though, instead of on this train so far from home.

I kept remembering the near-escape I had before I got on the train. Even though our family had told the Germans I would go to the labor camp, the Germans had to find each one of us. We knew that, and I planned, along with friends, to hide from them and stay home as long as possible. One day I confided to Aunt Paula that I would be the one from my family to go to the labor camp. Aunt Paula, who loved me so much, marched me out of the house and off to her church, where she whispered something to her priest and to the father of another family who was also at the church. Before I knew what was happening, the family had their bachelor son stand up with Aunt Paula and me before the priest, and he married us. "Now," said my aunt, "you are a married woman, and the Nazis will not dare take you!"

I was so scared and embarrassed at what was happening that I did not look up. To this day I do not know what the man I married looked like. I don't even know his name. I grabbed the piece of paper Aunt Paula pressed into my hand and ran for home to tell my parents. They were horrified. They would have done almost anything to keep me home, but even they did not dream of anything as extreme as this.

When the Nazis came to collect me, and we showed them the paper, it did no good. Many families had tried this; I was really going to have to go. I ran out of the house and to a neighbor's shed and hid in a haystack next to it. The German soldier pursued me and stuck a pitchfork through the stack a few times. He must have thought he had killed me, or at least frightened all the onlookers enough, and he just got into his Jeep and drove away. I was very much alive though, for each time the sharp pick had missed me. When the soldier left, I went home, determined not to hide any more. I wished now, as I stood limply up against the rest of the people in the boxcar and remembered that day, that the pitchfork had pierced my heart. Anything would have been better than this living death.

I didn't die on that trip, though others did. Toward the end of the journey, each time the train stopped and we were let out, the guards would drag out the unconscious or dead bodies and dump them in the ditches beside the track—no burial, no tears. Even the fellow prisoners were glad only for the extra space and the extra mouthful of food. We were beyond the physical and mental ability to think or care about anything else except our own animal existence. Jennie and I got beyond noticing each other, or whispering. We were like programmed robots who were unaware of the other human machines beside us.

One night in May of 1942 the train stopped for the last time. Trucks were lined up at the station to transport those who had survived the journey to the work camp. Mechanically I got off the train and into a truck. I do not remember how long we rode before pulling into a military camp. When the vehicle stopped, and the guards shouted an order, I nearly fell out. Was this the work camp, then? Perhaps the fresh air revived me, for a new alertness caused me to take in the whole scene with the curiosity of youth: barbed wire fences, strong floodlights shining from wooden towers and making the yard as bright as day, guards with machine guns in every tower, and hundreds of filthy people being pushed and shouted into some semblance of military order.

Men and women were lined up separately, and taken by groups to a dining hall area, where we were handed a can of steaming thin soup—the first and only food given us by the Germans on our lengthy journey.

After our meal, we were marched to another building where we were ordered to strip to the skin, and to throw our clothes into a pile. Then we went to large shower rooms, but the luxury of the shower was cut short by a male guard. With the bayonet on the end of his rifle, he prodded us toward a group of medical men who examined us quickly for physical defects and lice. How good it felt to have something warm in my stomach, and to have a clean skin. But then we were required to go back to the huge pile of clothing, find our cast-off clothing, and put it on again. Now that we were clean, we hated those filthy clothes even more.

We were herded back to the trucks, never knowing the name of the place where we had stopped for our soup, shower, and medical examination. Sometime later that night we arrived at another camp area, which apparently was to be our final destination. Here we were issued a prisoner number, a set of gray prison undergarments, a coarse, gray prison uniform, and a pair of wooden-soled sandals which much resembled our clogs of today. I answered a few questions, which were recorded on some sort of an individual record, and went back out into the yard to wait until all the hundreds who had arrived with me went through this initial processing.

We had arrived before the Germans were quite ready for us: as we were marched to our quarters much later that night, we passed long barracks under construction. The building in which we were to be housed was never meant to be lived in. The huge warehouse, which also seemed to have just recently been built, had nothing in it but a cement floor, four walls, and four toilets partitioned off on each end of the room—two for men and two for women. We were dead tired, and when the German guards shouted another order and some of the people lay down on the floor, the rest of us followed quickly.

The cement was damp and cold, and I slept fitfully, awaking to imagine the swaying and lurching of the train. But that was over. The moans of those around me did not make me feel less lonely, and I would fall back to sleep to dream of home. Each time I woke to disappointment—I was not home, but in a barn of a building filled with strangers. I hadn't even seen Jennie since we got off the train.

Soon I didn't want to go back to sleep. I began to pray as I had heard my father do so many times. "O Lord, save me; have mercy upon me," I cried. But I had no confidence that He heard me. My heart was sick and selfish. The disillusionment I felt made me cry to God for a temporary physical relief, but there was no repentance in my heart for my rebellion. There was no thought of the ugly crucifixion my Lord had suffered for me. All I could think of at this moment was my own suffering, and my prayer seemed to hit the warehouse roof and bounce back.

A siren made me jump, startling me out of the deep sleep into which I had finally fallen in spite of myself. As the guards shouted words that I could not understand, I stood up, crying out at the soreness and stiffness of my muscles.

This was the first day of my life at the work camp. What lay ahead? I was not to have much time to think about it. Already the day had begun.

8

The Camp—A New Home

---------------------- ✳ ----------------------

...the dark places of the earth are full of the habitations of cruelty (Ps. 74:20).

The Meldorf prison camp was to be our home for three months—or so we thought. At the time, we had no idea of our geographical location. I know now that Meldorf is approximately fifteen miles north of the mouth of the Elbe River. Hamburg, the nearest large city, is about fifty miles southeast. About ten miles north is a smaller place, Heide. We had no idea that just a couple of miles separated us from the coast of the North Sea.

The war work to which I had been assigned was labor in a large vegetable canning factory. Eight hundred of us would work here six days a week, around the clock in two shifts. One shift started at 6:00 A.M. and ended at 6:00 P.M., when the other shift took over. At first, my shift was the day shift, and we were wakened by the siren at 5:00 A.M. We formed lines again, and took our turn in the washrooms, where we were given two clean, empty lard cans. One was large, probably a ten-pound size, which we were to use to get water for personal hygiene. The other, a small can that we kept attached to our belts at all times, was for drinking water, for receiving our morning and evening tea, and for our noontime soup.

There were no sinks in the washroom, and no soap.

However, there was a large barrel of disinfectant just outside the washroom door. I grabbed a fistful of it, and rubbed it on myself. I desperately wanted to be clean. It must have had lye in it, however, for when it was combined with water, it burned unmercifully. There never was enough time for all of us to have an adequate turn at cleaning up, and sometimes it would be days or weeks before I had a good turn. The body and head lice became unbearable.

By 6:00 A.M. we had to be at the factory ready to punch our cards. Punching a time card was certainly not to keep a record of the number of hours we worked! Instead, it was just one of the means by which the Germans kept track of their eight hundred prisoners. Other means were posting guards at every entryway of our dormitory, and making daily bed checks.

On our way to work, we stopped by the dining hall to get our breakfast of tea ladled into our can. This we drank on the rest of our walk to the factory.

At the factory we were given an outer garment somewhat like a raincoat made of the same stiff prison-gray material as our uniforms. We put this on over our regular clothes to keep us a little cleaner at work. In some jobs and during some months of the year, it also helped keep us warm. The wooden clogs became a blessing because the floor was always wet and leather shoes would have rotted. More important, our feet always would have been wet.

The factory itself was a huge brick building built beside a railroad siding. Farmers delivered the fresh vegetables to the main door to be processed. The door at the end of the assembly lines opened into the boxcar waiting to take the processed food to the German armies.

There were different rooms for different processing methods: one was just for making sauerkraut; another for drying vegetables; still another packaged fresh vegetables; and last, were the actual canning rooms.

I worked in all the rooms during my stay in Germany. Some days I helped unload the wagons; others, I washed the freshly dug vegetables that some other prisoners unloaded. I remember how heavy those huge, steel, bushel-sized buckets got when filled with vegetables. My twelve-year-old arms ached and ached until I got used to lifting and carrying them—but we never complained. Complaining could mean a beating, and our German guards and supervisors carried three-foot-long rubber hoses for that very purpose.

Sometimes my job was peeling vegetables by hand. My fingers got very calloused doing that, and it was a monotonous job, but it didn't take us long to learn that it was better than lifting and washing the buckets of vegetables. We coveted the easier jobs—the ones where we could sit down, even if we did have to peel steadily for twelve hours.

One job I remember especially well was in the onion room. The onions were brought in in three-hundred-pound bags and we girls had to peel and chop them. My eyes watered so badly they swelled shut. I could barely see through the little slits. My clothes smelled so strong I could never get away from the odor of that room. It nauseated me constantly. I guess I could have stood it if I had not been so weak from lack of food, but the soup and tea and occasional black bread (we were given a slice of bread and a teaspoon of jam on Monday and Friday nights) was just not enough to give me the strength I needed for the grueling work day.

I learned to move quickly too, at whatever job I did. We each were given a shift quota of vegetables, processed and accounted for. If we didn't reach our quota (and often we didn't because it was set too high), we would lie about the amounts. Sometimes this worked, but sometimes it didn't because people on the boxcars kept their own record. If theirs didn't equal ours, a check was made. If we came up short, we had to spend Saturday evening until Monday morning in the camp jail, sleeping on straw. We didn't like this because we looked forward so to our free Sunday. However, it was better than a beating, and at least we could rest. The quotas also kept us from stealing vegetables to eat.

The summer was almost pleasant, compared to the freezing winter. The vegetables themselves were cold, the factory was cold and drafty, and with so little movement, our hands and feet would get numb. Those were the days we prayed for a transfer to the boiling vats or the drying ovens. The girls who worked in these areas took the peeled and cut-up vegetables and dumped them in the huge vats filled with boiling water. Then they emptied them out onto large trays which went on conveyor belts into the electric ovens which dried them. At the other side of the ovens they were packaged, counted, and loaded into the boxcars. Sometimes I worked on the ovens in winter; sometimes in summer. But always, winter or summer, good job or bad job, we waited for the noon and 6:00 P.M. sirens.

At noon, we had a half-hour break to get our can filled with thin soup made from the vegetable peelings left in the factory. Sometimes the soup would have a little meat in it when one of the horses died in the camp. We called it "garbage soup," but we were so happy to get it. After eating we would use the toilets and rest for the remaining few minutes. That half-hour went so fast.

At 6:00 P.M. we were anxious to get back to our beds. On the way home we would again pick up a lard can of tea and sometimes a bit of dried bread. But, oh, how depressing, when after our shift at the factory, we rushed out, only to have guards line us up and march us to the coal trucks. Coal was used to produce the electricity to run the machines of the factory, so it was vital to the operation that we never run out. There were few men around to do this unloading work, and with so many of us it went quickly, even though we had already worked twelve hours. After we unloaded the coal, basketful by basketful, we were so tired we would drag ourselves back to our warehouse, wipe our faces on our clothes, and fall into bed. I have never known such weariness, before or since.

Early in our stay at the camp we were lined up in rows and made to dig trenches. The Germans told us we were digging them as bomb shelters, but we never used them for that during the entire time I was at the camp. As we were digging, I recalled the terrifying sight in Kiev of trenches being dug for the Russian Jews, and soldiers shooting them so they fell into the trenches. "Bomb shelters," the Germans told us. I was sure they were not, and I fully expected that when we were finished with them, we would die in the same way as those Russian Jews.

Anxiety and fear were always with me. I could feel it in the pit of my stomach. The guards and supervisors told us what to do and how to do it. Then they would take us by the shoulder and give us a shake and say, "Understand? Then do it!" I never dared ask questions—but did whatever they told me. If I made a mistake, I was struck with the hose. I learned quickly. Once I was beaten for walking too slowly to work.

I was always looking for a friend. Once I thought I had found one. We weren't allowed to talk with our German civilian supervisors, but one woman who directed our work watched us with kind eyes—at least they looked kind to me. One day as she was eating her lunch, I saw her lay one-half of her sandwich down beside one of the machines. It was beautiful brown bread with thick slices of cheese and meat on it. My mouth began to water. She saw me staring at it, raised her eyebrows at me, and left. I just knew she meant me to have that piece of sandwich. I rushed over and grabbed it and divided it with the other prisoners who were working nearby. It was gone in seconds. Then she came back and acted as if it had never happened. Time after time she shared her lunch with us secretly, and I could never speak to her to say thank you!

Another woman supervisor broke her sandwich up into pieces and left them in her brown bag so if it was discovered she could say she was throwing it away. She turned her back as we reached into the bag and devoured the pieces. There was plenty of food in Germany, but they starved us, and some of the supervisors couldn't stand to see us suffer that way.

I was better off than my Polish friends though, for I had already been living under starvation conditions in Russia. The Polish prisoners had been well fed until they were brought to the camp. We all lost a great many pounds, but because I was a child and still growing, my bones seemed especially large as they stuck out of my tightly stretched skin. There was very little flesh in between.

A constant source of fear in the factory was the rats. They were always present, fighting for the refuse we would have loved to have. Nights were the worst with them, and I dreaded that shift.

Finally, in spite of the difficulties and danger, we were reduced to stealing. The older women would tuck potatoes into their clothes and smuggle them back to the warehouse. We would wait until dark and crawl out the bathroom windows with our tin pails full of water and run in the darkness to the trenches we had dug. I hated it, but I helped. We had collected little piles of scrap paper and sticks during our Sunday walks and placed them in the trenches. Now we found them and made small fires to boil or roast our potatoes. We then ate them with great enthusiasm. As I look back, I believe those midnight potato feasts were what kept me alive in my new home. We were always afraid of discovery; fear was a constant companion no matter what we did.

We feared the bombs that fell regularly at night. The sound of the planes was like the droning of a huge swarm of bees. We screamed, ran out into the field, and threw ourselves face-down on the ground. We cried and prayed through the noise. When it was over, the sky was lit up with fires everywhere. We never had a direct hit on the factory or on our barracks, for which I was thankful. I remember shaking all over for the few minutes the planes were overhead, which seemed like hours. But what really hurt was my stomach.

At first I thought my stomachache was just from being in a new place with new foods. As the pain grew worse and worse, I thought it must be because I was so hungry. But when I began to vomit blood and pass it through my digestive tract, I knew, young as I was, that there was something seriously wrong with me. I had never heard of stomach ulcers before, but no doubt this was the problem from which I suffered (I still have them today). I didn't dare tell anyone in charge, because I would have been taken away. Others who had become sick and were taken away were never brought back. Most of us believed they were dead. As bad as the camp was, I didn't want to be taken away. The unknown was worse in my mind than the known. So I suffered and lost weight, but kept going; partly because of youth, partly out of fear, and partly because of the encouragement of fellow prisoners.

On Sundays, when they shut down the factory to clean it and repair machinery, we had a welcome rest. Only a few were assigned each week to clean, and because there were eight hundred of us working in the factory, our turn to clean did not come too often. We would clean our bodies instead, and try to clean our clothes. The only soap we had was the disinfectant used to scrub down the toilets, which was kept in a barrel beside the toilet door. We took a handful secretly every time we went into that room, and used it in some way to try to get clean and kill the lice that had stayed with us from the filthy boxcars. We hung our washed clothes near our bed so no one would steal them, or in warm weather, we laid them out on the grass to dry. We took turns wearing each other's clothes while we washed our own, and the one from whom we borrowed stayed in bed to hide her nakedness.

Also on those precious Sundays, we walked around the camp yard for fresh air and exercise. The camp was enclosed with an electric barbed wire fence. At intervals along the wall were little houses on high platforms from which armed guards constantly watched the fence and the entrances and exits to the camp. It was on those days that I realized more than ever that I was a prisoner. I was used to hunger, fear, and hard work in Russia, but to be herded like a huge pack of animals in a small enclosure, and to have to look at the world of trees and grass and sun through barbed wire, made me weep and long for freedom— even the limited freedom of a Communist state.

9

Prisoner— A New Way of Life

✳

Let the groaning of the prisoner come before You (Ps. 79:11).

By the fall of 1942 our permanent barracks were ready. We had passed them daily on our way to work in the factory, and eagerly awaited their completed construction. The cement floor of the warehouse was damp even in the warm weather and there was little privacy. The winter was drawing near and we longed for warmth.

The barracks were long wooden buildings with eight small dormitory rooms housing twelve to sixteen girls each. An armed guard stood or sat by each of the doorways to the outside to observe anyone's leaving. The bathrooms had sinks, toilets, and showers, but still no soap.

Each dormitory room held four bunk beds, four bunks high, reaching almost to the ceiling. On each bed was a straw mattress and one gray prison blanket. To those who had lived in the warehouse for three months, it was pure heaven. The beds were clean; the wooden building was not damp; the smaller number of residents per room gave us a sense of closeness and intimacy—a family unit—and there were more toilet facilities, which was a luxury. It was an exciting change in our drab life.

One of the special joys of moving to the barracks was

that, by some miracle, Jennie and I were assigned to the same room. For a long time after we moved in, we just sat and looked at each other because we couldn't believe it was true. We became closer and closer as we shared the prison experience.

Also, just after we moved I received a letter from Maruska. I was so happy and excited as the guard handed me the envelope. She had sent me a picture of herself and when I saw it, the tears ran down my cheeks. I wiped them away with my fists and eagerly began to read the letter, but the news quickly erased my happiness—the tears flowed again. She had been taken prisoner soon after I left, she wrote, and sent to a camp in Vienna. My father had been taken prisoner along with her and also was somewhere in Austria, but she didn't know where. She didn't know what had happened to my mother and little brother. She closed by asking me to try to meet her after the war was over.

I was in a state of shock after that letter. My dear father in prison, too—Mother and Kolia left alone to support themselves in German-occupied Russia. I began to pray; the prayer became my daily ritual. "Lord, let the war end. Let me live just one more day." Over and over I prayed, "Just one more day, Lord."

Then I received a letter from my father in a camp in Austria. He wrote: "I miss you terribly, Tania, and I pray for you constantly. If you get this letter, please let me know." I wrote back to him, but I never heard from him again. I kept his letter close to me all through the war. It was a part of my father—the only part I had left.

More prisoners arrived that winter of 1942 from Russia, Poland, Holland, France, and Lithuania. One in the new group had been a neighbor of mine in Kiev and brought me news that there was hardly anyone left in my family. I don't know how she knew about my family since they were so scattered, but the news discouraged me again.

Jennie and I never let the guards know that we were friends and even hid our happiness when we were assigned to the same dormitory. We were afraid they would find some way to part us. Somehow we managed to live together for three years. Some of the others in our dorm were old enough to be our mothers and our grandmothers, but I became close to them all.

I remembered Father's words of counsel at home, and tried to be the girl he would want me to be. The older women seemed drawn to me, and when I would talk to Jennie about Jesus, they would listen. Jennie was Russian Orthodox and wore a cross and prayed a lot. This made me feel even closer to her. We talked and talked about Jesus. We talked of our families too. She loved to sing and I would teach her the songs our family had sung at home about Jesus. We shared everything. We had good times together and bad times. One particularly bad day Jennie asked me, "Tania, what would your mother do if she were here, cold, hungry, tired, and afraid, with bombs falling all around?"

I said, "She would sing this song:"

> Don't worry, poor soul inside;
> Don't worry and get discouraged.
> Remember the Lord remembers you;
> In His time He'll undertake for you;
> Right now in Him you hide.

If only I could have really believed the song and lived it! The song was true, but still I worried, and got discouraged. My body couldn't take it.

As winter wore on, the pain in my stomach became unbearable. Some days I would lie on the floor and scream from the cramping until I vomited. I began to think I would not live to see the end of the war. Jennie prayed for me and comforted me, and again, just in the most desperate moment of my life, God worked a miracle.

In June 1943, the prison officials chose twelve of us girls, including Jennie and me, to go to a German resort on the coast of the North Sea. Our job was to work in the kitchen and dining room, serving German officers and enlisted men who were on leave for rest and relaxation from the war. They took us by train to the resort town and we met Frau Swartz, who was the owner of the resort. Hans, the manager, was responsible for our security and training. He took us to a little attic room and hung a number around our necks. It was hot in that attic, but it was clean and private and quiet. Each of us had a bed and towels and linens and soap—wonderful soap. Best of all, we had access to more and better food, and my stomach healed that summer.

Our job was to serve in the dining room and clean the tables after the soldiers had eaten. Most of the leftover food was saved for other meals, but the food the men left on their plates was scraped into a pan to be given to the chickens. I thought to myself, *The chickens are eating better than we are.*

Though we were watched carefully in the hotel, when we took the garbage out to the chickens, we would grab the largest scraps and eat them before we went back inside. Sometimes we fought with the chickens for the food.

Frau Swartz told us with tears in her eyes that she wanted to treat us well (and she did treat us better than we had been treated at the camp and in the factory), but she was being watched and couldn't take the risk of being thought a sympathizer with prisoners or disloyal to the Nazis.

We enjoyed the change and rest of that summer; especially our little private room. It was in this room that Jennie received Jesus as her Savior at my invitation. Strange that

I could help her while still rebelling in my own heart against God.

We wrote letters home and gave them to Hans, who promised to mail them for us. They were never returned, so we lived in the hope that they had been received by our families.

Fall came too soon and we went back to the camp and our work with the vegetables. I was assigned to the boiling kettles, and one day while lifting a lid, I received a steam burn from my wrists to my elbows—the only parts of my arms that were uncovered. Involuntarily I cried out, but when I saw others (including the guards) looking at me, I quickly flipped my apron up over my arms and smiled. I did not want to be taken from the camp. Back in the barracks that night, I cried the tears of pain I hadn't dared cry before. My friends bathed my arms in cold water, the only treatment we had. As prisoners, we were never given any medications. I wore a long-sleeved, white blouse to cover my arms while they blistered and drained and finally healed. It was very painful, but I never let anyone except those in my own dorm room know about my injury. After the war we heard that the sick had been shot and burned in huge ovens, but mercifully we didn't know that at the camp—our imaginations were bad enough.

The guards ordered us around, pushed us, pulled our hair, and were in general as rough and mean as they could be to us, whenever they had opportunity. One especially mean guard slapped us across the face if we didn't understand him quickly enough. We were beaten with rubber hoses and imprisoned for minor offenses, but we were spared one cruelty. No one sexually molested us. We heard it happened in other camps, but, somehow, ours was free from it. In fact, the guards acted as if we were an inferior race—not good enough for them to be interested in—and we were glad. Husbands and wives who had come to the camp together were housed separately and assigned to different work. They seldom got to speak to each other—just occasionally if they passed on the way to work. I thought we were treated terribly, but I know now it could have been worse—at least I lived through it, when some did not.

The second winter, 1943, went faster for me because I looked forward to going back to the resort. Hope is a wonderful thing. For amusement during the winter, we saved scraps of brown paper from the factory and rolled our wet hair into curls. When it dried, we had new hair styles. We combed each other's hair and caught each other's lice. By now the straw mattresses were a year old, and our clothes were not coming clean when we washed them without soap. Lice and bedbugs were everywhere.

We had found ways of taking salt from the black barrels in the factory and used it on our fingers to brush our teeth. If we couldn't get salt, we used sand. We had no dental care in prison, and the pain of a toothache had to be borne like any other pain.

The spring of 1944 came, and some of the older girls didn't want Jennie and me to go to the resort again. They put in a complaint to the guards. We wouldn't have gone, either, except that Frau Swartz asked for us especially, and we struggled to control our joy. I was very glad for Jennie's sake. She hadn't been feeling well all winter, and I was worried about her.

Again that summer we had our little attic room, hot and cramped, but blessedly clean and private. Frau Swartz was so good to us that summer. She gave us each a skirt and blouse, and we wore them under our old ones so no one would know we had them. As she gave them to us she put her finger to her lips and we didn't speak. Hans brought each of us a dress from Frau Swartz one day, and then took us on a walk down by the sea. We usually couldn't go for walks, except to empty the garbage. Sometimes it was so hot that, even though we were dead tired from working from dawn to dark, we couldn't go to sleep. The cool walk by the sea did wonders for us.

When Jennie seemed to be getting weaker, I decided she would feel better if she had some bread to eat. The food was kept in a locked pantry, but it had a high narrow window which was always open. I took a chance for Jennie, and crawled through it into the room. A woman coming to work saw me. She told me later she just *had* to report me because she was afraid Frau Swartz would blame her for the missing food. They caught me in the pantry. I was afraid I was in for a beating, but when they called the Gestapo, I became frantic. Would they shoot me for stealing a piece of bread?

They took me just two houses away to where a Gestapo officer lived. While I was being interviewed, the officer's two little children smiled at me and played at my feet. I loved children, and I smiled back and played with them. The officer's wife watched me. She must have been thinking what a child I was myself. Anyway, she talked to her husband privately before he told me my punishment. She must have pled for me, because he let me go free with just a severe warning.

I hurried back to Jennie. She wasn't much better, and she was anxious over my long absence. We struggled through the summer with Jennie's getting weaker and weaker, and my trying to do some of her work and giving her most of the food. But food didn't seem to help. Soon after we returned to the camp in the fall, Jennie got so sick she couldn't get out of bed. I begged and begged her to get up; I knew she would be taken away if she didn't. But she couldn't, and one day it happened. The guards came and picked her up in a truck, and I never saw her again. I was filled with despair. It was the lowest point of my whole time at the camp.

I lost track of time and lived hour to hour, day to day, as the winter of 1944 dragged on. It was so cold that winter, we slept in our clothes and with other prisoners. Sicknesses of all kinds swept through the entire camp. They finally brought us new straw for our mattresses and burned the old ones to try to stop the epidemics.

We lost all our dignity and humanity, and lived like animals. We hardly knew the difference between day and night. We had no calendars, and we heard no news. We didn't know what most of the rest of the world knew—that the Allies had landed at Normandy in June and were steadily marching from the west toward Germany. On the Eastern front, the Russians routed the Germans from their land and held the Polish front from August to January.

As the spring of 1945 dawned in all its splendor in the outside world, there was only winter in my heart. It never occurred to me that in every desperate moment of my life in the past, just at the worst time, God had stepped in with a miracle to save me. I looked forward to no new miracle. I was bitter toward the Germans and the Russians and my parents. I asked again, "Why was I born?" I had no hope for the freedom that was just days away.

10

Liberty Brings Hope Again

✳

...the LORD has anointed Me...
To proclaim liberty to the captives,
And the opening of the prison to those who are bound
    (Is. 61:1).

It was May 8, 1945, and I was fifteen years old. I got up just as on any other morning, not realizing right away that there had been no siren. Habit is the best reminder, and the camp was going about its routine without being forced. When I went out in the hall to go to the bathroom, I noticed there were no guards at the door, but that had happened before. Since we had gotten into the routine, we were left alone more often in the barracks. The guards always had been nearby, outside the door, so I paid no special attention.

It did seem cold in the building. I touched the steam radiator and it was cold, but that wasn't unusual either. Seldom did we have any heat this time of year. But there was no electricity, either—that might explain the missing siren. We talked about it in our dorm room and decided there might have been a major power failure. So we went about our duties and lined up to march to the factory. Strangely, there were still no guards! It was deathly quiet in the camp.

It seems now that we were dumb, but we had been expecting nothing. Our hope had died long before. We scarcely had enough strength to hold up our heads and look around. What was there to look for, anyway?

We shuffled toward the factory somewhat more slowly than if the guards had been there, a little apprehension added to our depression. We were so regimented that we did not even talk to each other, though there was no one there to beat us for it. All was deathly silent. All at once it hit me—the trenches! We were going to be led to the trenches and shot and buried in them! This had been my constant fear since I had seen it happen in Russia. But it had not been quiet there: people had screamed and cried and moaned and gasped for breath—and prayed.

I knew there was something unusual about the camp, but my dulled, unexpectant mind couldn't comprehend it. No one was in the dining room where we usually got our morning tea. *Another trick,* I thought, *to wear us down. Another cruelty, to reduce us to subhumans.* It didn't matter. I didn't feel the hunger anymore. The steady pain in my stomach was such a part of me, I never associated it with food or hunger. It was the normal way to feel now.

We went inside the factory and lined up for our jobs. But here, too, there were no guards, no supervisors, and no electricity. We looked about carefully. Were they hiding, ready to jump out at us if we tried to escape? With no power, we couldn't work, so we just stood in the order of our barracks and waited. Minutes grew into an hour and an hour into two. Still, years of fear kept us waiting. Finally those near the door heard something and looked out. There were soldiers entering the camp in Jeeps and trucks; there were American and English flags. The word spread, and finally the doors swung open as the soldiers drove up.

Then everything broke loose. Everyone screamed and cried and shouted and ran to the trucks and kissed the men and danced around. Sudden new hope had given us an energy we never dreamed possible. The soldiers threw us bread and canned food, and we grabbed it, shouted with joy, and broke it into pieces to be shared all around.

Then the soldiers motioned us all over to the big building the Germans had used as a dining room and headquarters. As we all crowded into it, an officer stood up on a table and began to speak. Several people of each nationality translated for us into Russian, German, Polish, Dutch, and French. The message was that Hitler was dead, and the German high command had officially surrendered to General Eisenhower and General Montgomery two days before, and the official documents had been signed the day before. The Russians had occupied Berlin. The war was over. The Allies had won—and we were free.

For a moment everything was quiet; then the noise started all over again. Inside and outside, radios began to play music and everyone danced and sang. People searched through the crowds for husbands and wives they had not touched for years. Soldiers questioned us about our treatment, and told us stories of scenes in other camps that had been liberated. The day flew by.

I left the crowd and walked slowly back to my barracks alone. There in the quiet and seclusion of that place that had become home for me, I wept tears I had forgotten I had in me—tears for all the suffering; for the release from fear; for Jennie, who had died too soon; for my father, who at this moment was probably being freed in Vienna; for my lack of faith and hope; and thanksgiving for my new freedom. I don't know how long I cried, but my friends came and found me after dark. They bathed my face and combed my hair and took me back with them to the building where the music was still playing and the dancing and singing and celebration had just gotten into full swing. I stayed awhile, but I didn't dance. I talked to the soldiers and answered their questions. I listened to them tell of camps so much worse than ours—particularly the camps for the Jews. I asked them about Austria and how long it had been in Allied hands. They didn't know, but they assured me it was a free land again.

The lights from the Jeeps and trucks made the prison yard bright. We walked around the yard and through the gates. Though they were open and there were no guards, no one left the camp. Where would we go in a strange land? Perhaps we would run into Germans again outside the gates.

I got very tired and, with some of my friends, went back to our dormitory. None of us could sleep, but we talked and laughed and made plans all night. Some of the women didn't come back to the barracks that night at all, but stayed at the mess hall and celebrated. Some were reunited with their husbands and went to their barracks with them.

The next day we rested and talked and took showers, trying to make ourselves as presentable as possible. The American soldiers shared their food with us, making a stew that tasted wonderful! There wasn't a lot, but they promised us more. None of the Allied soldiers abused us in any way. I heard stories later of these things happening, but it was not true of our camp. They were good and kind to us, and helped us all they could. The officers in charge of the soldiers in our camp were older, with families of their own. We loved to talk to them; they were kind and we told them all our troubles as we would our own fathers.

Soon the camp became better organized. The Allies furnished the food for us. The actual cooking was done by the Germans, with our assistance. We were given two meals a day to begin with. The best treasure of all was a whole loaf of bread each week for each of us to keep to snack on. Because there were so many of us, our food distribution times were staggered. Some of us were issued our loaves of bread on Monday, and some on Wednesday. We shared with one another and had plenty of bread to begin to build up our physical strength. Most often we ate our loaf up before the end of the week, but we didn't care. We knew more was coming and we were starved.

The International Red Cross sent in clean clothing, and each of us could choose a dress. We didn't know or care about styles. I picked whatever fit me and was colorful. Only later, when I got to the United States, did I realize my dress was for an older woman.

After everyone had chosen one dress, we took turns choosing until we each had two. There were no underwear or coats available, but when the soldiers issued each of us a khaki blanket and some woman found an old sewing machine, we all got busy with scissors and needles and thread and soon every woman in camp had a dull green coat or jacket. What luxury!

The soldiers gave us soap, toothbrushes, and toothpaste, and we laughed and enjoyed each new treasure. We got different foods, like canned meats and powdered milk. When we got bold enough to venture outside the camp, we would take these new treasures to a German farmhouse, and trade them for other things we wanted. I got a pillow that way and thought I had never slept better than that first night with my head pillowed again.

Every night we would celebrate again. The soldiers took us for rides in the Jeeps around the camp. That was the first time in my life that I had ever ridden in a vehicle for pleasure. We somehow acquired flags from each country represented in the camp, and put them up in the mess hall. Then each national group would get up and sing their national anthem and do their folk dances. Everyone else would clap and shout approval. Patriotism ran high.

The Allies also set up an office, an emergency medical

clinic, and a dental service right at the camp. We all took turns getting needed attention. I remember my first visit to the dentist—I had nine fillings at one sitting. There was no Novacaine, so I had to endure the drilling. When I screamed, the soldier said, "I'm sorry; I know it hurts, but I'm here to help you." At that moment I thought I could do without that kind of help, but I was grateful for it later.

I signed up at the clinic for a doctor's appointment about my stomach. When they had a truckload, they would announce over the loud-speaker the truck's time of departure for the doctor's office in Hamburg. I was able to see a doctor about my stomach pain and bleeding. I had had intestinal bleeding from my ulcer for a long time, but now the bleeding was from my female organs. The doctor told me I needed more care than he could give me right then, and gave me a prescription to use as a temporary measure. But, when I went to the German pharmacy, they knew who I was—a liberated prisoner from the camp—and didn't fill my prescription. They kept it for their own people because there just wasn't enough to go around.

With this new awareness of illness came anxiety. Time was going by and the celebrating was dying down. I longed to see my family again. I was glad to be free, but free to do what? I was still a prisoner in a way. There was no place to go—I was still at the camp.

11

Freedom to Go Nowhere

❋

"Our bones are dry and our hope is lost" (Ezek. 37:11).

After a few short weeks the Allies got the camp organized again. The United Nations set up an office to help us find our families. They interviewed each of us, asking where we were from, where, and for how long we had been in prison, and what our future plans were. I was ready for that interview. I wanted to find Father in Austria, and I wanted to go home. Somehow I had thought if I ever got free that I would walk right out of prison and go home. What a childish dreamer!

The interview itself seemed to be forever in arriving, although I really didn't have to wait long. All kinds of identification measures had to be taken with each of the eight hundred persons. I was impatient.

When I came in for the interview, I saw on the desk the information sheet with my name. I also saw on the sheet the notation "born August 29, 1929." My eyes grew wide with wonder. August 29! It was the first time I had ever been told the date of my birth. In Russia, a baby's birth was designated only as early or late in winter, spring, summer, or fall. I knew only that I had been born in early fall. We did not celebrate birthdays in Russia. And during the war, none of the prisoners ever spoke of birthdays. So this was a novel bit of information about myself, and I treasured it.

My hopes of returning home to Russia were high, but I was to be disappointed. My counselor didn't discourage me outright, but he warned me so I would begin to face reality. Word had been received that Russian prisoners of war who worked in labor camps were considered traitors by their country, and were not welcome back in Russia. Some who had returned had been sent to Siberian prison camps.

What a blow! To live for three and one-half years with the desire to see home and family again, only to have this ironic twist. *Only the Communists could have thought of this,* I mused in my bitterness. I don't know what they were afraid of, but perhaps they thought we had become indoctrinated with bourgeois philosophy. Maybe they felt it would be too difficult and expensive to deprogram us. They might not have wanted to bother with citizens in such terrible physical shape. Whatever they thought, right then I knew that people as individuals were not important in the USSR, and after all I had suffered, this blow seemed hardest to take. To live with a hope for years and have that hope sustain you through unbelievable hardship, only to have it blasted in a moment by the only national ties you have in the world, is devastating to the mind. And knowing that breaking that national tie means breaking all family ties crushes the spirit. No wonder the interviews took so long—the counselors had to pick up the pieces of the lives of people interviewed and help them put their world back together.

The United Nations workers wrote letters to the camp in Austria, but could find no trace of my father. I believe he must have died in that camp. He seemed to have vanished without a trace. There were no prison records for Paul Awdienko. It was almost as if he had never existed. If I hadn't had a letter to prove he had been there, I might have believed that myself. That letter was the last contact I ever had with him. I carefully kept it with my personal possessions; but one day when I looked for it, it was gone. I was heartbroken. And his wallet, my last physical link with him, became even more precious to me.

The officials checked for my mother and Kolia in Kiev, but found no information concerning them. Uncle Nikoly was no longer in Kiev. They tried to trace Uncle Ivan and Aunt Paula in Mikhaylovsky. They were not able to locate Aunt Matya in Odessa, or Aunt Nastya in Tolokun. There was no way they could check for Uncle Dannis in Rybolov. It was as if my family had completely disappeared, or as if they had never existed. I wondered if they had all been taken by the Germans to concentration camps. Perhaps they had died. I would never know for sure. Brokenhearted, I realized I would have to give up the search. I slowly reconciled myself to starting a new life alone. But where?

The counselors offered a variety of countries—Australia, Canada, Brazil, Argentina, and the United States of America. I thought a long time before I decided. I remembered the kindness of the American men who liberated our camp. I remembered what my countrymen had said about the United States—that it was a bad place to live, and the people there were our enemies. If Communists thought that, then it was probably a good place to go. This was the way my mind began reasoning. So I chose the United States for my new home. The next question was, Would they have me?

When I told my counselor my decision, he told me what it would mean. They would look as carefully as possible into the kind of person I was. My name would have to be changed to Awdienski, a Polish ending. My birthplace would be changed to some town in Poland and my birthdate changed to four years earlier to make me four years older than the fifteen I really was. I didn't care anymore what happened, just so someday, somewhere, I could start a new life out of the camp as a truly free person. I still cried each night for my lost family.

One day I woke up with a sore throat. It seemed to be swollen, I had a fever, and my ear hurt. I had to wait for a bed in the hospital for two or three weeks. In the meantime they treated me at the camp clinic, but by the time I could be admitted for hospital care, I had begun to feel better again. It seemed good just to have people who seemed to care, to listen to my problems again. Many little things about the camp began to change slowly.

My friends and I had begun taking walks out into the German countryside as soon as it was allowed and considered safe. At least we felt a little freer, even though we couldn't go far. The farmers we met called us *ost,* a new name meaning "displaced persons." Although we talked to them often, we never felt very close to them. When we told them how we had been treated, they had nothing to say. Perhaps they didn't want to believe us, or maybe they were waiting for the German prisoners of war to return and report on their treatment before they sympathized with us. Some gave us sandwiches to take home with us. My mouth waters even now to think of those German sandwiches—one thick slice of brown bread wrapped around slices of meat and cheese. During the war, our diet merely had kept us alive. Now we were enjoying two meals a day. But anything homemade was a very special treat.

They also gave us old garbage cans which we took back to camp and cleaned out for laundry tubs. It was a luxury to have clean clothes and clean hair as often as we wanted. We got rid of the lice first, and we wouldn't let anyone who wouldn't keep clean in our room. We had had enough of those bugs after three years.

I was surprised the German people never talked to us about Hitler. I think many of them were still afraid. They didn't really know who were Nazi loyalists, and they were taking no chances. Also, no one really knew for sure what had happened to *der Führer.*

After a while we knew the neighbors well enough to help with their farm work, and we also hunted for fuel in the woods for them. The farmers came to the camp when they needed help, and we would go with them. In return, they gave us home-cooked meals, fresh vegetables, and homemade bread. It was such a joy to be in a real home again. Often they would make us sandwiches to take back to camp with us, but we always ate them on the way. There was no end to our hunger.

After the war the Germans bought and sold with government trading stamps, so there was no way they could give us any money. But they gave us what they could, and we counted them as friends. Before our long wait as displaced persons was over, our lives would become even more intertwined.

One day news spread through the camp that Russian soldiers were visiting each barracks looking for citizens of the USSR. I couldn't figure out why they did this if they really didn't want us. Were they afraid of the tales we would tell to the Western world? After the information given me by my counselor, and the stories I had heard from other prisoners, I knew I didn't want to go back.

The Russian soldiers soon walked into our barracks unannounced and came into my dorm room. They began their inspection by smiling at us and saying something in Russian, such as, "Hello, girls; how are you?" They were watching closely, of course, for any sign of recognition of what had been said. Anyone who appeared to understand, or who gave them a reply in Russian, revealed the fact that she had come from Russia. Those women were immediately taken away by the soldiers.

I tried to appear casual when they came past me. By this time, I was quite proficient in the German language; but I knew I had to pretend not to understand what they were saying in Russian. Along with the others in my dorm room, I gave them a blank stare, never allowing even my eyes to betray that I recognized the words. They were clever, but I had determined to be even cleverer. I kept priding myself on my acting ability while they were there, but when they left, I couldn't stop shaking with relief. One might wonder why they had not come to each room to see who "looked" Russian, but Russia is such a large country, with so many ethnic groups, that there is no "typical" Russian look.

The camp began to empty rapidly. Most of the French and Dutch prisoners were able to go home shortly after our liberation. The Poles and Russians stayed the longest. It was hard to get information from our countries, and many of us were so young. I think also the countries who were taking people from behind the Iron Curtain—from Communist countries—wanted to be sure we had the right motives in wanting to come to the free world. Whatever the reasons, our days as displaced persons stretched into years, as they had as prisoners. My stay in Germany after the war was to be five years almost to the day, from May 8, 1945, to May 1950, when I left for the United States.

To pass the time, when we weren't working on German farms, we worked at the camp. A few of us were in the kitchen each day and some cleaned the barracks and the public buildings. Others picked up paper and rubbish and burned it.

It was also a full day's work to pick up enough wood to

make a fire to boil water in our garbage cans to do our laundry each week. We were given soap by the Allies, and we used it as we boiled our clothes to get them clean. Then we carried them to the river to rinse them and lay them out on the ground or on tree branches to dry.

For recreation we went fishing with poles made from tree limbs. I didn't catch many fish because I was afraid of putting the worms on the hook. Imagine living through a Nazi camp and being afraid of worms! A German woman who had supervised us in the factory during the war came to visit us one day and gave us an old bicycle to use. We took turns going for rides in the countryside. I had never ridden a bicycle before, but I learned quickly and took my turn. The first time I went on a seven-mile trip and almost killed myself when I turned over going downhill.

We spent some time on personal hygiene each day, and we made over clothes that were given to us and practiced giving new hair styles to each other. Many people were good to us, and we didn't know how unfavorably our life compared to much of the Western world, because what we had now was so much better than our lives as prisoners. We were thankful to be displaced persons.

Time passed for us much faster than when we had had no hope, no freedom, and little joy. But I soon found another way to pass my time.

12

The Displaced Persons' Christian Church

That he might present it to himself a glorious church (Eph. 5:27).

One Wednesday after supper someone said to me, "There is a group praying in the dining room." My first inclination was to say something like, "Oh, yeah. So what?" But I didn't know those expressions then. Instead the thought bothered me. I remembered again the words of my father, "People who love God will meet any time they can to worship Him and pray!"

Why am I not with them? I thought. *Why haven't I heard of them before? Don't I love God?* My mind continued the conversation with itself. All the old feelings from childhood in Russia flooded in upon me. Why was I born into the world if all I was to know was suffering? How could there be a God who really loved the world and me, yet allowed disease, starvation, kidnapping, war, murder, and loneliness to exist in such abundance? I remembered my friend Jennie. She died without ever seeing Liberation Day and the subsequent freedom she had dreamed of for three years. It just wasn't fair. I didn't want to worship or pray to a God like that.

Father's words again broke in on my bitter thoughts: "Promise me you'll meet me in heaven, Tania. There is nothing sure but that place. There is no hope but that hope."

My mind answered, *Isn't the United States of America a real hope?* Then another thought began to plague me: *Maybe if I don't go to the prayer meeting God won't let me go to the United States.* My concept of God was a huge Father-type in the sky who rewarded me if I was good, and withheld good from me if I was bad. Somehow I had internalized the feeling I must be really bad to deserve all I had been through since I was born. This feeling of unworthiness made me uncomfortable when I thought about the little group of people who were in the dining room praying. But the thought drew me there like a magnet. The very next Wednesday I attended the meeting in the dining room. It was both a spiritual exercise and diversion.

The small group of displaced persons who led the service and brought messages from the Bible were Christians from different barracks in the camp. They had discovered one another after the liberation, when they were finally allowed to visit freely other barracks and discuss any subject.

A Russian-speaking Pole led more often than any other, serving as a kind of lay pastor. We sang hymns accompanied by a harmonica. They prayed, and I prayed, too, like the rest. I guess I thought if I acted like them, I would *be* like them. I was so afraid and insecure in my relationship with God, that the first time I prayed aloud I fainted in the middle of my prayer. I knew nothing of repentance. Nevertheless, I felt better being with the Christians than being away from them, and I soon became an enthusiastic supporter.

With all this fellowship, I still wasn't satisfied. It didn't seem to be enough for me. If I was a child of God then, I do not know; but I did not feel close to Him. The relationship I had with Him was not enough. I was lonely and longed for some close human relationship here on earth. I didn't put it into words, but it was in my mind.

Many of the other girls who were waiting with me for final clearance of papers and passage to a new land had found lovers among the men in the camp, and married them. I watched this with fear and hope in my heart. I had always been a little afraid of men, except for my father and uncle and brothers. The sight of them brought to my mind acts of cruelty, and I was always suspicious of men I did not know. The men connected with the oppressive Communist rule and the German occupation and labor camp filled so many years of my young life, that I had very limited experience with kind men. I actually thought that God had made a mistake when He made men—that they were something to be avoided. So I never talked to them. Even when the American soldiers came to liberate our camp, I let the other girls do most of the talking to them. In the church service, I listened and talked only with the women.

One day, however, in the dining room at the camp, a tall, dark, handsome, quiet-mannered man sat next to me and tried to talk to me. I ignored him, as was my custom, not proudly, but shyly and fearfully. He kept trying to get me to talk to him, and I began to feel like a hunted animal wanting to run. He somehow sensed my fear and began seeking out my girl friends, getting to know them. He asked them questions about me, and they told me everything he said. "He likes you, Tania," they would tell me. "He thinks you are pretty. You really ought to talk to him and get to know him," they urged.

I tried to still the fast beating of my heart and keep the red flush from my face and the smile from my lips. But I was very human. I needed attention and love and it wasn't long until I would look at him and begin to answer his questions—at first just with monosyllables.

He began to come to my barracks every day asking for me, and I would go outside to talk. I remembered some of what my parents had taught me and would never let him into my living quarters. Soon we were going for long walks and eating our meals together in the dining room. Our friendship was growing. Not once did he try to touch me, but he told me often that he liked me, and he was very kind. I found out his name was Stephan and he was eleven years older than I. He was from Poland and although his parents were there, he felt there was nothing there for him since the war, and he was looking for a new land to call home. He even started coming to the prayer services because of me, and the people there welcomed him.

We spent more and more time together and the days flew by. Strange that marriage never even crossed my mind, when I wanted to belong to someone so badly.

13

Someone to Belong To

❋

"And the LORD God said, 'It is not good that man should be alone'" (Gen. 2:18).

I continued to see Stephan, and he often told me he loved me. One day he said, "Tania, I would like you to marry me. Will you think about it overnight?" I was surprised. I had never thought of marrying him. He was just a special friend. But I said I would think about it and I did. I thought all night. My father had talked many times about marriage to the little groups of people to whom he ministered in Russia. Much of his teaching flooded through my mind that night. I could almost hear his voice, saying: "The person you marry must be a believer in Christ. You must not take this lightly, for marriage is for life. Once you marry, you must live with that person the rest of your life."

I thought and thought: *All my friends are getting married. I will have someone to go with me to a new land, and I will never be alone again.* Then a new thought occurred to me: *But I don't love him; he is nice, but I don't think I feel about him like my mother felt about my father.* I determined to talk to him about this the next morning.

He came early to get my answer. I said, "How can I marry you if I don't love you? I don't even know if I know what love is!"

He smiled and replied, "I know you like me, Tania, and

you will grow to love me, so don't worry about that." He seemed more like a father to me than a lover, and perhaps that was what I was searching for right then.

It was a whirlwind courtship of less than six weeks. Had my parents been there to counsel me, I am sure they would have cautioned me to give myself more time to become acquainted and learn what kind of man Stephan was. But my parents weren't there, and I promised to marry him as soon as he could make the arrangements.

We applied to the person in charge of the camp and filled out the German legal papers at Bergedorf. Stephan had an old German silver coin that someone had given him, and he had it made into a wedding ring. On the given day, we stood before a magistrate and said our vows to each other in German. There were no music, no flowers, and no special dress—just Stephan and I, the witnesses, and the official in a bare German office. It was a very short ceremony, and I was not sure at any time that what I was doing was right. I only knew that for the first time in a long time there was another human being who cared about me, was kind to me, showed special attention to me, and wanted to spend his life taking care of me. After the years of suffering and loss, I just could not resist that strong emotional pull.

When we had filled out the legal papers to be married, we were assigned to a new barracks room, to be shared with two other couples. We hung up blankets for privacy, and in our section of the room, we had a bed, table, and a little electric hot plate to cook on. We had moved our things into the room earlier in the day, and I was excited about "playing house."

Just like many other things in my life, my marriage was wrong from the beginning. My husband had been married to a Polish woman and had a child by her. He didn't tell me this until after we were married because he knew that I would never have married him. That made me very sad. His parents had written him that his wife was unfaithful to him while he was at the prison camp, and since the war had married someone else. It was true when he told me, "I have no reason to go back to Poland," but that was only part of the truth.

Also, I knew little about sex. I had become a woman at the camp, without a mother's guidance and help. What I knew I had picked up from some of the women prisoners, but I still lacked much needed information. On our wedding night, when my husband tried to touch me, I began to scream. I had learned to live with the pain in my lower abdomen. It had come to be a normal part of life, but I could not bear the intimacy of marriage. It hurt too much. My husband quieted me with a promise that he would not touch me again until I was ready.

There were about twelve couples in our barracks, and they all knew there was a problem. Some of the older women tried to counsel me. For six long months I kept my husband from me. We talked, then argued, then fought. He started staying away nights in his frustration. He said he was fishing. At the same time, though, as our life became somewhat of a routine, I began to be happy. My husband was good to me, and we had some fun times with the difficult.

We went to help German farmers pick apples in their orchards, and were paid with all the apples we could carry home. We had to walk five miles and cross creeks to get to and from the orchard. Stephan would carry me across the creeks and help me on the walk. I was so happy to have someone care for me, that I think I began to love him a little for that. We would run up to the dining room together like children to eat our meals; at fifteen, I really was still a child. I would see my old girl friends and stay to talk and sometimes run off with them. Stephan would patiently call me back to clean off the table. I needed to grow up, and he was indulgent in helping me do so. When I think of how little girlhood I really had, I wonder how I ever made it through those first few months of marriage.

After six months of fighting and reasoning and counseling, my friends talked me into telling a doctor about my marital problems. The doctor, a kind man, examined me with great care and found my internal organs had been damaged by the heavy labor in the prison factory. In fact, some of my organs had been torn loose and had reattached themselves in new, wrong locations, causing great pain and bleeding. The answer was surgery. I entered the hospital in Hamburg and stayed for three weeks after the successful surgery. My husband came to visit me often. He must have loved me in his own way, and he was very kind and understanding.

As I was convalescing, I walked about the ward, talking to other patients. One time I saw a woman in a corner bed who looked familiar. It was Mary, an older woman from our barracks who had tried to help me by answering my questions. She lay in her bed, quietly reading a book, and as I approached her she looked up and smiled in recognition.

I asked, "What are you reading?"

"The New Testament," she replied with a gentle smile. I told her of my Christian parents, and she said, "Then can I call you Sister?"

I said, "No, I have lots of problems in me yet." I didn't know how to explain, and she didn't press me further. She just told me, "Tania, you know, I pray for you and will continue to do so." When I went back to the camp, the deep longing in my heart was still unsatisfied.

Mary and I became good friends after she returned from the hospital. She was like a mother to me. She and her husband, Nikoly, were White Russians from the area north of the Ukraine. (They later came to the United States, where Mary, eighty-six and almost blind at this writing, is still praising the Lord and looking forward to "going home" to see Him who has sustained her all these years.)

Meanwhile, the church group grew larger, and even some of the German people living around the camp came and worshiped with us. When they saw our fellowship, they invited us to visit their church. We took them up on that, but not until after a big moving day.

The displaced persons' church really took a spurt of growth when we Meldorf prisoners (those still awaiting placement) were transferred to Wünsdorf, a permanent Nazi army camp. We were packed into waiting trucks. We carried our belongings in our hands, so few they were. After about a half-day of travel, we reached our new home, approximately one hundred miles south of Meldorf.

The facilities at Meldorf had been temporary ones constructed of wood, except for the factory, which was there before the camp. Several of these temporary camps had been hastily built to house all the prisoners of war and workers. Now it was costing too much in time, money, and personnel to keep them all going. So all units in the area were consolidated at Wünsdorf.

The buildings there were of brick and concrete, and there were many rooms made available to us for our social and religious activities, as well as for more private living quarters. With the new facility and the larger population, the prayer group grew. We had as many as two hundred people worshiping together at the height of our fellowship. Finally we organized and called a pastor just like a regular congregation. The man we called was a White Russian named Golankski, and he organized and shepherded us.

The pastor arranged with the camp officials to have trucks transport us to the Lutheran Church in the town of Wünsdorf. It was a miracle to me to be able to walk into that church and see the white-haired German believers, singing the same hymns we sang. Just a short time ago they had been our hated enemies. Now, we were brothers and sisters of a common faith. The one thing Hitler could not stamp out was the miracle of the Christian church that unity could exist under such circumstances. We joined that day in a common favorite hymn, "God Is Love." Some sang in German, some in Russian, and some in Polish. What a mixture of guttural sounds, but what sweetness of melody!

The pastor asked me one day if I had been baptized, and I said, "Yes, as a child in Kiev."

"Oh, no," he said, "have you been baptized as an adult?" I had to answer no. Well, right away he made plans for a baptismal service in the river by the camp. I had had so little teaching that I didn't really know what "being saved" meant. I would do anything anybody told me to do to try and find the peace and assurance I knew Father had had. But baptism did not give that to me. I put on the white robe the pastor borrowed from one of the churches in town and went down under the water and came up just as empty and confused about my spiritual life as before. It was a formal service, read from a book. I was not asked to give a testimony, and it was a good thing I wasn't. I had none to give, even though I could have made up some good-sounding words. I still did not know of repentance, or commitment, or making Christ Lord of my life. I only had a part of the truth and it was making me miserable. Still, I could not forsake it all.

The German Christians told us of retreats to be held in Lübeck and Hanover. Pastor wanted us all to go. We had to go through the red tape of getting passes to leave camp overnight, passes to travel on the train, places to stay overnight in the city, and promise of food provided at the retreat site. But the adventure was worth it. Doing something different from our routine was a thought to be eagerly anticipated, and became a memory to be treasured and relived for months to follow.

All was arranged and we left the camp for two days and nights. There were hundreds of us gathered on the campus of a university in Hanover. We slept in the college dormitories, and ate in the cafeterias—food furnished by the Americans, and cooked by the Germans. We had services three times a day. In one, two sisters gave testimonies of God's help and comfort while they were displaced persons; in another we heard an American missionary speak; in still another our own pastor ministered along with pastors from other camps. The large volunteer choir sang beautifully and brought many blessings. Too soon it was over, and we left our new friends and the excitement of something new, and were sent back to camp.

When I had come home from the hospital free from pain, Stephan and I finally became one flesh. About a year later, after we had moved to Wünsdorf, I became pregnant. That began a time of more difficulty. I hemorrhaged throughout the entire pregnancy, and my husband again spent many nights away from home.

I spent my time preparing for the baby. I cut up old clothes to make seven diapers. We got Care packages of needed items from the Allies, and from some prisoners who had gone home. My husband saved the things in his packages and traded or sold them to buy things for the baby. In spite of problems between us physically, it was a rather happy time in our lives.

Finally, I went into labor, and my Kryssy was born on February 11, 1948—a healthy baby girl. Her father named her Krystina after his mother and sister. She was born in the camp infirmary with the aid of a nurse, and in a few days I took her home to our barracks room.

My baby became my life. I completely ignored my husband. Now I had someone who was truly mine, and I truly knew what love was. When she cried, I rocked her; when she wet her diaper, I changed her and immediately washed out the dirty one. I made all her food from the camp food on my own stove. I nursed her with milk from my own body. My baby was so precious, I could think of no one else.

My husband started going "fishing" again, as he had when we were first married. Only this time, people began bringing me reports that they had seen him in town drunk. Other rumors started that he was stealing from the Germans and selling the stolen goods to other Germans. I cried and the baby cried. Each time he came home, we fought bitterly. Soon he never came home sober. Our roommates left us because of the problem, and from then on, most of the time I was alone.

Because of my marital problems, I turned more and more to the prayer group to find fellowship and spiritual help. One blind man in the group prayed faithfully with me for my husband. When I heard his story, I knew why. When the war ended and everyone was celebrating, he and his friend had gotten hold of some "bad liquor." His friend died, and he went blind. Since then he had had a special concern for drunkards. I walked him back and forth to his barracks with his white cane. He held on to the baby's carriage, which a German woman had lent me, so he wouldn't stumble. We became good friends.

I never missed going to the group now, especially since I could pour out my troubles to this older man who seemed concerned about me and my husband. Others in the group helped me, too, encouraging me and praying for me. I tried to be like them. I thought I was a good Christian as they were, but in my heart I knew there was a difference. Nothing I did was natural for me; I had to try harder. I knew deep in my heart that I wanted God to help me in my troubles. In fact, when things were going well, I didn't go to the group for fellowship. There was no repentance for my sin—no life commitment. There was only conformity to outward patterns, and no one seemed to recognize this or challenge me about it. At the prayer meetings I would pray for my husband, and for my life to be different. For the little while I was there I had hope, but when I started home despair flooded over me, and I was sad again.

Other girls in the camp had their own marital difficulties. One of my friends from the barracks in Meldorf had married a man twice as old as she. Maria used to tell me some of her problems, but she seemed to tell my husband more. During one particularly bad time in her life, I invited her to go with me to a picnic the church was sponsoring. Since she lived a few miles away, I said she could spend the night with us. How very naive and foolish I was—such a little girl yet. I watched her and Stephan flirt and enjoy each other all night, ignoring me. All the hope I had for our marriage seemed to dissolve.

Early the next morning I was to go to a farmer's house nearby to get some potatoes to fix for the picnic; if I was not there early, I might not get any. I told Maria the night before, so she would watch Kryssy, but I didn't tell Stephan. We weren't communicating too well anyway, and he looked for any excuse to stay away from home. He had just come home, and I didn't want to upset him.

A friend had lent me a bicycle and, as I pedaled, I cried and cried. Drinking and stealing were bad enough, but the thought of another woman was too much. I didn't blame Maria, but I blamed him. He had said he loved me. *This is love?* I thought bitterly. I shook all over. After I bought my potatoes and went home, Stephan and Maria were gone. Another woman was watching Kryssy.

I took her to the picnic and found comfort and sympathy with my friends. However, something strange happened to my husband that day. When I came home, he was waiting for me. He seemed truly sorry and asked me to forgive him. He explained that these things he did were a part of his family life in Poland, and he didn't think of them as wrong. "After living with you," he said, "I know they are wrong." He even prayed that day. I could scarcely believe my ears.

During the following days he stopped drinking and stayed home and helped me. He did seem different. I remembered my father's words again, "If you marry the wrong person, you must stay with him for life. Marriage is for life!" So I forgave Stephan, and we started over again.

I tried to stay a friend to Maria on the surface, but in my heart I rebelled against her and was very hurt. Soon she left with her husband for Argentina, and although I wrote her once, I never received an answer. Another woman, who knew us both, told me she heard that Maria left her husband as soon as they got to South America. I just wanted to forget it all. Something new was just ahead that would make me forget.

It was almost time for our departure to a new land. Five years had passed since the Americans had liberated our camp. It was 1950. My new life of freedom was about to begin.

14

A Long Trip Home

✳

He also brought me out into a broad place (Ps. 18:19).

Our papers were all in order and approved; a sailing date had been set. We went for our last physical examination to make sure none of us had communicable diseases. To my dismay, the doctors found Kryssy had a fever and put her in the hospital. In the two years since she had been born, my baby had never been away from me, but the experience was more painful for me than it was for her. We both cried as they took her from me.

I hung around the hospital for a while trying to figure out a way to be near her, finally becoming a volunteer in the hospital. I went directly to Kryssy's room at the first opportunity. We hugged each other and cried some more. When a nurse came in and found me, she ordered me out. For the next few days I did my volunteer work and spent the rest of the time under Kryssy's second-story window. I would talk to her until she fell asleep, and then I would fall asleep myself. I was thrilled when the fever broke and she was released. Then we were ready to travel.

We had our choice of plane or ship, but I chose the ship because I was afraid of airplanes. Imagine living through what I had and being afraid to ride on an airplane.

Everything happened so quickly that we were on the

train going to the seaport before I was aware our applications for the United States had been finalized. We had nothing much to pack, so it was easy to leave. I said a few goodbyes to the people at the camp and to some of the German Christians, and took my most precious possession, my own little German citizen, Kryssy, and followed my husband on the trip to my new home.

There were twenty-four hundred of us to board the ship. The men and women were separated just as in the early days of the camp. We were way down in the bottom of the boat. Because I was busy caring for Kryssy the first few hours on board, I never knew when we left the shore. Soon I began to get this strange feeling in my stomach. All I could think of was, *I've got to get off the boat a minute.*

When I told the other women, they laughed and said, "Look out the porthole." I did, and saw nothing but water. I had the strangest feeling of being trapped.

I got sicker and sicker as the day went by. My husband had a job on the ship as a patrolman, and I seldom saw him except as he made his rounds on his eight-hour shift. But when I got so sick they had to put me in the ship's hospital, he had to care for Kryssy. She began to run a fever again, and by the time we got to Ellis Island, New York, we both had to be taken off the ship on stretchers and transported to the hospital there for immigrants. I was thin and weak, and desperately anemic. The baby had German measles.

My husband was detained in the men's dormitory on the island for three weeks while I was given blood transfusions, medication, good food, and rest. I couldn't believe the food they gave me—not just three meals a day, but snacks in between. When they came in the evening with the beverage cart and asked if I wanted milk or juice, I answered, "Both!"

The nurse laughed and said, "Of course you can have

both," and each night thereafter I drank both milk and orange juice. I had never tasted orange juice before in my life, and I loved it.

I gained strength quickly and was glad finally to be released and walk out on my own two feet. For a long time I had been lying down. On the boat, when they hosed down the sleeping areas for sanitary purposes, they had rolled me out of the way. I had been so sick, I hadn't cared if I died. But now I cared. I was ready for life.

Our train tickets had been sent by our sponsoring family, and the immigration officials took us by taxi to the depot. I felt strange, knowing no English. It was as if I were still in prison in my mind, while my body was free. I began to look around for all the things people had told me about the United States. My father had often longed to go to this land, for he had heard people could worship openly anywhere they pleased—even on the street. He had said the Bible was an open book here and verses from it were printed on billboards lining the roads in America.

My friends from the camp who had come here earlier had written us about the abundance and variety of things one could buy. But I could read no English, so the billboards were a mystery; and I had no money, so I could not shop in stores. I could only ride in a taxi to a depot to travel to a farm in Kentucky to work to repay my passage to this land.

Is this what it is like to be free? I asked myself. People were still directing my every action. I was afraid again. *What will happen here?* I anxiously kept asking myself over and over again. I was faithless. I had lost faith in countries, in men, in marriage. I didn't trust anyone. I lived only for Kryssy. Everything else I did mechanically, because I had to.

Lots of displaced persons traveled on the train with us to Adairville, Kentucky, which was a focal point of immigrant activity. Adairville is southwest of Bowling Green and just north of the Tennessee border. Sponsors went there to pick up their immigrant workers and then fanned out throughout the entire state with them. Our sponsors, Mr. and Mrs. Slaughter, were there to greet us and take us to their farm about three miles from Adairville. They seemed pleasant enough, and smiled and pointed to the waiting car.

We drove in silence for about ten minutes, except for Kryssy's baby chatter. Mrs. Slaughter tried to communicate by sign language and smiles that she liked the baby, but I just held her closer to me. I looked out the window to see a green countryside rushing by.

At last we pulled up in front of a square, dirty, white box of a house in the last stages of disrepair. It was stuck up in the air on four ugly stone pillars, and some of the windows were boarded up. The outside pump and toilet reminded me of Russia. I took it all in in one glance, and didn't like what I saw. I might have resisted getting out of the car if I had had any other choice, and if there had not been four familiar faces rushing out the door of that house to greet us.

Sonya and Wladiek, a family and their boys, we had known well in Wünsdorf, were already at this farm, working off their passage. They had told the Slaughters about us and had urged them to bring us to America. They also had offered to let us live with them if we could come. Here they were in front of the house to welcome us. We would live together, sharing everything except their bedroom.

After much hugging and kissing, I went into the house with Sonya to look at my new home, while the men stayed outside. Mrs. Slaughter followed us in, still trying to communicate with me. Sonya could help now. I learned they wanted us in the fields at 5:00 A.M. the next day, and, as a friendly introduction to the farm, they wanted to show us the fields we would be working.

It didn't take us long to get our few things into the house and into the bedroom that would be ours. Then the Slaughters took us out for a ride in the fields. They seemed endless to us—over eight hundred acres. The broad-leafed tobacco plants were already a good size. We drove past the Slaughters' big house, surrounded by many other weather-beaten buildings, and then back the one mile to our house. By that time Sonya's two little boys and Kryssy were crying out their tiredness, while the rest of us showed it in our drawn faces and sagging shoulders. However, we were not to have even a day to rest or settle in. The last thing the Slaughters did before leaving us alone in our new home was to show us the alarm clock and explain how to use it. They offered graciously to let one of the women stay with the children at home until 10:00 A.M., when the truck would pick them up and bring them to the fields.

We all were relieved when they finally left, and we were alone. We broke out in the Polish language, all speaking at once. Wladiek was Polish, like Stephan, and Sonya was Russian, like myself. Whenever we didn't want our husbands to know what we were talking about, Sonya and I would speak in Russian. We had learned to speak some Polish for our husbands' sakes, and since it was the language of the camp, we all spoke German. We laughed and we cried at our reunion—laughter that we finally had found familiar faces in a strange land, and tears because of the lack of freedom we still felt as immigrant workers. Gratitude for a place to stay and work, and for the privilege of a chance to start out a new life in a new land, was mingled with indignation at the early working hour, the requirement that both women work and bring the children to the fields, and the lack of time to catch our breath and become acquainted with our new surroundings. However, we were used to taking orders, and 4:00 A.M. found us jumping out of bed to the ringing of the alarm clock. With two families working together, we could easily be ready for the truck's arrival at 5:00.

That first morning the three of them went off to the fields and left me at home with the sleeping children. At 8:30 Mrs. Slaughter came over to take me into the small town and introduce me to the general store. I learned we could charge our groceries and pay at the end of the week. I had never heard about this before—the concept of credit was new to me. I didn't dream then what a trap it could be for a family. I picked out a few things I thought we would need, and Mrs. Slaughter had the man write it down on a bill. I was amazed again when we walked out without paying any money.

We went back to the house and I made up some sandwiches and a bottle of Jell-O (we mixed it with water and drank it like a soft drink). Then she drove me to the fields where the others were. I took the children with me. Sonya, Wladiek, and Stephan were as glad to see me as I was to see them, both for the sandwiches, and for the security of all being together in this new place.

I was immediately introduced to the green tobacco worm which insists on chewing holes in the beautiful green leaves of the plants. It was Sonya's and my job to pick them off the plants and kill them. Here again I was strangely fearful. I laughed at myself as I remembered the starvation in Russia, the boxcar ride, the labor camp, and the ocean voyage—and I was afraid of a little green worm! Foolish as it seems, I never did get comfortable with those soft, squirmy things in my fingers or under my shoe as I stepped on them, but I did my part anyway. Sonya and I also took turns watching our three little children. When they got tired, we put them on a blanket in the shade and they slept contentedly. When we moved to a new spot in the field, we moved them with us.

The day was long, but if it had ended at 4:00 or 5:00 P.M. and we could have had our evenings free, I think we would have been happy. But there was supper to get for the two families—Sonya and I did that—and our men had to help with the evening farm chores—milking cows and feeding pigs.

That night when it was dark and the four of us were sitting out on our front steps to rest in the cool evening breeze, Stephan and Wladiek told me what our salary would be for working here—a dollar per day per person. It didn't sink in right away, because the dollar was a new thing to me. I would have to learn by what I found a dollar would purchase at the general store. Along with the twelve dollars a week per family, our house, utilities, furniture, transportation, milk, and garden vegetables would be given us.

We were satisfied with this. In fact, we felt happy and rich. At least we had no guns pointed at us; we could keep ourselves clean; we had privacy and a little leisure in the evenings and on Sundays; we would have enough to eat to keep well and grow strong; and we were used to working hard. We only had to stay for six months and our passage would be worked off. Then we were free to go anywhere we wanted—that is, if we were careful and didn't charge too much at the general store.

We smiled at one another in the darkness, and began to make plans to better our living conditions. We dreamed and dreamed as we went over the house carefully room by room. Later we would dream of a life apart from this house, but now our dreams were centered here.

15

My Old Kentucky Home

✳

"The LORD has brought me home again empty" (Ruth 1:21).

Our house in Kentucky had four rooms—living room, kitchen, and two bedrooms. The floors were wide wooden boards worn bare of paint or varnish by years of use. I can't remember any color in the house at all in either the furniture or the walls. The kitchen had a white table and chairs with peeling paint, a cupboard, a wood stove, an old icebox (with the ice-keeping section taken out) used as another cupboard for food, and a wood box. The living room had old overstuffed furniture with holes in the upholstery and sagging springs, a couple of brown tables, and a heating stove. Each bedroom had two beds, a chair, and nails in the walls with hangers on them for our clothes.

There were a few dishes in the kitchen, enough silverware to give us each a spoon or fork, a skillet and two pans in the drawer of the stove, and a wash basin on the cupboard. How Sonya and I wanted to fix up that house! The men just wanted us to cook for them and let them sleep at night. After we were there awhile, we got to know some people who helped us make our house a little better, but none could make our pitiful dreams come true.

On some days Mrs. Slaughter would have Sonya and me come and work for her in her home. We washed dishes, made butter, washed and ironed clothes, scrubbed floors, and dusted furniture. While dusting I once dropped an antique vase and broke it. I begged Mrs. Slaughter to let me pay for it, but she only replied wearily, "No money can replace it." Even so, she seemed to like me better than Sonya and kept asking me more and more often to work in the house. Sonya was quite outspoken and had been there longer. She and Mrs. Slaughter had had a few problems before. I was new and anxious to please, and glad to get out of those fields, away from those ugly worms.

At night, when the Slaughters had card parties, she would have me come to the house, make popcorn and lemonade, and serve it to her guests. Once she asked me to make a Russian meal for the family. I decided on cabbage rolls, and Mr. Slaughter loved them. Mrs. Slaughter seemed to be bothered that he liked them so much, and she told me they were too rich and upset her husband's stomach during the night. I felt sad again. I really wanted to please and keep my privileged place.

For those extra hours of work, Mrs. Slaughter would give me old clothes for myself, and some to remake for Kryssy. All this time Sonya was doing extra duty baby-sitting. That was the hard part—being away from Kryssy.

When Sonya and I worked together, we would sing songs in Russian that we had learned in the Displaced Persons' Church, where we first had met and become friends. When we both married Polish men in the camp, and each had a child within the next year, we thought of ourselves as more than friends—something like twins. We were very close. Mrs. Slaughter loved to listen to us, and once she went to her piano and played the music for the song we were singing. I thought surely she must be a Christian to know that song. How little I knew about being a Christian. Yet I came to see that many people were just like me, thinking people were Christians because of what they did (or didn't do) or what they knew.

I was reinforced in my thinking on Saturday when Mr. Slaughter invited us to go to church with them the next day. Sonya and I went, taking the children, but Wladiek and Stephan stayed home. Perhaps they thought they would feel strange in that church because they were of another denomination, but I think they wanted time to rest and put in our own garden.

We made many new friends at the little church where they took us, and many were especially kind to us. It was here we saw how out-of-style our clothes were, and the people brought us lots of their castoff clothing. They gave us each a patchwork quilt, and I almost cried at the beautiful colors. They pressed silver coins into our hands, and some, like our neighbor, Mrs. Tiflin, brought over dishes, silverware, and other household goods until our house began to be much better equipped.

After a few weeks, the pastor of the church asked us to become members and be baptized. Sonya didn't want to because she had been baptized in Germany. I think she knew much more than I did about being a Christian, and right then she didn't feel she was living up to all she knew. Our husbands, who had started attending church with us, weren't interested; but I was. I had kept in contact with our camp pastor, who had come over ahead of us to the United States. He had settled in Chicago, and I wrote him about being baptized. He wrote back, "You've already been baptized; you don't need to do it again." But I didn't listen to him. The need to do something to be approved and accepted within a group was strong. And there was that awful knowledge inside me that I was not right with God. Doing this one more time might just be the answer. I was always looking for easy answers. Oh, how I longed for peace with God, but I didn't know where to find it.

Mr. and Mrs. Slaughter thought it was a great idea for me to become a member of their church, even though they didn't attend as regularly as I did. I suppose they felt a little like missionaries in this endeavor of influencing their immigrant workers in going to church. So the date was set, and on that Sunday I was baptized for the third time—and for the third time I came up out of the water knowing nothing of the work of regeneration in my heart, realizing nothing of the significance of what Christ had done so I could stop trying to justify myself by my works.

After I was a member of the church, Mrs. Slaughter began taking Sonya and me to her church ladies' meetings once a week. She would have us sing and talk a little, and the women thought it was wonderful. Sonya didn't want to sing and talk, and soon Mrs. Slaughter began leaving her at home to work. I learned to sing, "God Bless America," and it became a big hit with everyone. The best part of it all was that the women usually had a very good lunch and would give me lots of the leftovers to take home. Each week on that one day, Wladiek, Sonya, Stephan, and our children would watch for me to come home with pies or cakes or cookies or salads, and say, "Good girl, Tania!" But I began to feel guilty about Sonya's having to be home working while I had an extra afternoon off each week. She knew that Mrs. Slaughter preferred me and there was tension between us. I finally told Mrs. Slaughter I could go with her only once a month. That limited our special treats, but the harmony between Sonya and me returned, and that was worth far more.

Every two weeks the Slaughters would take us to the general store, and we would have a chance to spend some of our money on staple foods. The cheapest and best for us were corn meal and sugar. On my first shopping trip I was fascinated by the pictures on the canned goods labels. I bought a large can of peaches for a quarter, and the others bought their own treats. I could hardly wait to get home to taste mine, but I forgot one thing—we didn't have a can opener. Stephan took pliers to the can while I found a spoon. I let everyone taste a slice of peach and a little juice, and then I sat down and ate the whole thing. Never had I tasted anything so good in my life.

Sonya became an expert at making corn bread, and it was our only baked goods except when I went to the ladies' meeting. One August 29, a lady from the church came to our house. She had heard it was my birthday and she brought a big, decorated cake. We all stood around and admired it. It had candles on it and letters in frosting that said, "Happy Birthday, Tania." We didn't even know what it all meant because we hadn't celebrated birthdays before. She explained the custom of birthday parties in America, and left with Sonya's reminder ringing in her ears: "My birthday is in November."

On one of our first trips to the store, each family purchased a large wash tub. We used them for washing clothes, and once a week we took turns taking a bath in them. We would heat up the water on the stove in buckets, and dump it into the tubs outside, behind the house. We had a great time splashing and not getting the house dirty while getting ourselves clean. It was so warm there was no danger catching cold. But all good things must come to an end (my philosophy of life then), and someone must have seen us and thought it indecent. Mrs. Slaughter came over one day to tell us we had to bathe inside the house. Because we had no privacy at the camps, we were almost insensitive to the rigidity of the propriety in the United States. Those six months in Kentucky were indeed a time of learning for us all.

None of us had been able to drive, but both Sonya and Wladiek learned in the fields of Kentucky. That way, no one had to pick us up for work, for one of them could bring an old farm truck home at night. They didn't have licenses though, so we never could go off to town alone. Perhaps this was good for Stephan. We almost had forgotten the bad times in our relationship in Germany. When I thought of Maria and how it was rumored she had left her husband to move north to Canada, I just prayed she would never come near Kentucky. Stephan had been very good to me and Kryssy since arriving in America. He worked hard and long and had no transportation to town, so he never drank anymore. I was beginning to really love him as we shared more and more of life together; however, more and more, we were beginning to see that we would never get ahead on the farm here.

Soon after our six months with the Slaughters were completed, we got a letter from a displaced person who had settled in Wisconsin. He was a tailor, and had been in the church group with me at the camp in Germany. After working off his sponsorship he had gone to Neenah to look for work and had found an abundance. He wrote, "There are lots of jobs here that pay good salaries. You should come!"

We also got a letter from Stephan's uncle who lived in Stevens Point, Wisconsin, asking us to come and stay with him and look for work. It all sounded exciting. Stephan and I talked it over with Sonya and Wladiek. They wanted to go to Detroit, Michigan, where other displaced persons we knew had settled, but both Stephan and Wladiek had to wait until the final tobacco harvest work was done. So we decided that I would go on to Wisconsin and stay with the uncle and look for jobs for Stephan and me. Then Stephan would follow in three weeks or a month. It took lots of courage, but I was young and foolish and adventuresome. I was also tired of working so hard for so little.

The day came when we broke the news to the Slaughters. They were upset. Mr. Slaughter promised to raise our salary now that our passage to America was paid off. He told me I was upsetting his wife very much because she depended on me and I was a good worker. He also said she liked me. I knew she did, and I felt sad, but I knew we would never get ahead and be independent in Kentucky.

My neighbor, Mrs. Tiflin, who had given me the household goods earlier, now brought me a hat box into which I packed all my things and Kryssy's. We hadn't accumulated much in those six months. She told me also that she would treat us very well if we would come and work for her. But our minds were made up—we were bound for Wisconsin.

We had a written invitation for housing from our uncle who was an established home owner. We had enough money for Kryssy's and my train fare saved. We had the promise of help in locating a job; and we had the will to succeed. We had everything we needed officially and personally to move.

It was hardest to say goodbye to Sonya and Wladiek. The United States was such a big country, and we had just found each other and grown close again those past few months. But dreams of making lots of money, the miracle of many transportation systems, and the will to see each other again gave birth to promises that comforted us as we said our farewells.

Mr. Slaughter drove me to the train depot while Stephan stayed behind working in the fields. We had said our goodbyes earlier, and a month seemed such a short time to wait after all the other waiting I had done in my life. Mrs. Slaughter wouldn't say goodbye. She was angry that I was leaving, but she also thought that I would soon be back. I felt very lonely when I boarded the train and waved for the last time to my sponsor. Even though I felt they used us in many ways, they did show they cared, and they were our first friends in a new land. As with my father, I would never see them again.

16

A Sojourn in Wisconsin

✳

"I am a foreigner and a sojourner among you" (Gen. 23:4).

I had a ticket to Stevens Point, but right from the beginning I had determined not to go there. I didn't know Stephan's uncle, and I did know the young man in Neenah. Both had promised to help us find a job, so I thought either place was as good as the other. I still had much to learn.

The ticket agent in Kentucky had told me exactly where the Traveler's Aid desk was in the Chicago depot. He was right, and some of my fears subsided when the woman at the desk communicated to me that she could speak German. She was helpful and got me on the right train for Wisconsin when it was time. During our wait Kryssy and I ate the lunch I had packed for us. When we went outside for a little walk, I noticed it was much colder than in Kentucky. I began to worry that it might be colder yet in Wisconsin. We had no warm clothes; we had known only intense heat in Kentucky and never had occasion even to wear a coat. The warmest outer garments we had were sweaters. There was not much time to be too concerned though, for they were calling our train.

As the steam engine huffed and puffed its way through the countryside, Kryssy slept and I made my plan. I would get off at Neenah. If I had any problems finding my tailor friend, I would change trains for Stevens Point. I knew nothing of the geography so had no cause for worry at that moment. As the hours passed it began to dawn on me how alone I really was, far from Stephan and Sonya and Wladiek.

I began to notice white patches on the ground, and before long the entire countryside was covered with a white blanket of snow. I hadn't seen snow since I was in Germany, and it made me homesick. I began to cry softly. The conductor noticed me and must have thought I needed help. I had told him I was stopping at Neenah, and when we got there he took me by the arm and led me to the depot office. I was afraid then. The uniform and the strong arm brought back bitter memories. The combination of weariness, loneliness, and fear made me completely fall apart emotionally. All I could do was say my tailor friend's name over and over in a heavily accented voice, broken with sobs. The people in the office finally distinguished what I was saying and called my friend on the telephone. He said, "Yes, I know her, but I didn't know she was coming and I made no arrangements. I live alone in one room—I cannot take her in."

I didn't want to get back on another train and try again, and I didn't speak English well enough to explain about myself and my plans. I cried and Kryssy cried, and the officials finally took matters into their own hands—they called the police. Soon more uniformed men came in a car and motioned for me to go with them. I bowed my head and prayed in Polish. I was so afraid. Again I seemed to have no control over my life. Was it always to be like this? Finally I followed them.

The cold, late fall night air refreshed Kryssy enough that she stopped crying and started asking questions. "Why is it so cold, Mommy? Where is Daddy? Where are we going,

Mommy? When are we going to eat? Where are we going to sleep?" Her questions had a quieting effect on me, and my own tears subsided as I comforted and answered her.

The police had put a call through to the radio station and an announcement had gone out over the air asking for someone to take a refugee woman and child in for the night—preferably someone of Polish descent. It didn't take John Kulkowski long to arrive at the police station to pick us up. I hesitated about going with this strange man, but the police had checked him out and smiled and said, "It's O.K.; it's O.K." I understood that American word, so I went along. Besides, what choice did I have? I had little money and a language barrier; I had a ticket to Stevens Point, but I didn't know which direction the station was, and I was dreadfully cold in spite of the blanket the police had thrown over my shoulders. At this point I just let people lead me. Mr. Kulkowski spoke to me in Polish, and that gave me confidence to get in his car.

When I got to the Kulkowski home and was met with a hug by his wife, I was glad I had gone with him in spite of my fears. The lights and warmth of the house, and the warm, loving acceptance of the people soon made me feel very much at home. These people were amazing. They explained to me in Polish and some German that their daughter had gotten married that day. The festive appearance of the house and the table loaded with all kinds of holiday food had made me wonder. But after all that celebration, they were still willing to come after a poor refugee woman and her child and take them in. I was sure they must be Christians, too.

John led me to the table while his wife, Patty, took charge of Kryssy. They loved each other right away. When John brought a big plate and began serving me, the tears came. How could they be so good to me, a stranger? Kryssy began to cry when she saw me crying, and I had to stop. "Mommy's crying because she is so happy, Kryssy," I explained.

After we ate, I told my story in part, and the Kulkowskis assured me they could and would help me. They were kind, even apologizing for all the dirty dishes in the kitchen and around the room. I laughed then—it seemed funny that they should apologize to me for anything. If they could only have seen the old white house in Kentucky, or the single barracks room in the German camp, or the warehouse, or the boxcar in which I had lived over the past eight years, they would have been the ones to laugh at the contrast with this lovely home of theirs.

I slept like one dead that night, with Kryssy nestled close to me in a bed with clean, white sheets and warm quilts. What luxury—luxury I had never known in my life except in the hospital. I woke to the smell of food cooking. I washed and dressed, and to my astonishment, I found I had slept fourteen hours, and it was noon of the following day. No one had wakened me.

I spent the rest of that first day getting acquainted with my new home by helping Mrs. Kulkowski clean it up. We walked and talked while we worked. She told me about her three children, Bob, Teresa, and Paula. Bob had been married for a while, but didn't have any children. Teresa had married right out of high school a year earlier, and Paula, a foster child, had just been married the day before. Patty said, "I'm lonely now with all my children gone. Will you stay here, Tania? Will you be my daughter and let Kryssy be my first grandchild—at least until your Stephan can come?" I couldn't think of anything I'd rather do, and thanked God for the blessing of this home. "Call me Ma, Tania," Patty said, "and call John Pa. He'll like it." I determined to stay in the Kulkowskis' home and help them all I could to show my gratitude for not only giving me a home, but a second family as well.

Within the week John found me a job as a hotel maid. I changed beds all day long with an American high school girl, for twenty-five dollars a week. Then I hurried home to vacuum and dust the house I called home. Patty took care of Kryssy for me, and I never worried a moment about her. She really did treat Kryssy as her own grandchild. She also helped me write Stephan, and in three weeks, around Christmas time, he joined us at the Kulkowski home. They welcomed him as they had me, and we could scarcely believe our good fortune.

Stephan found a job immediately at a foundry for fifty dollars a week. We thought we were fabulously rich. Right away we began to give the Kulkowskis money for room and board. They didn't charge us much, because I was doing housework such as making the men's lunches, scrubbing, and general daily cleaning. They didn't charge us anything for babysitting Kryssy either, so we had money left over each week. With it I began to buy some new dishes, silverware, and bedding. We bought new clothes, and even had some spending money left. I spent my allowance on candy, potato chips, and ice cream. I loved them, and couldn't seem to get enough.

Then Mrs. Kulkowski got very sick and had to stay in bed for many weeks. I stayed home to take care of her. She taught me to play cards and bingo, and bought a large supply of malted milk balls for us to snack on while we played. I played as long as the candy lasted. While we played, Ma taught me English. This was my school of American studies.

Our first Christmas was exciting. We got a package from Mrs. Tiflin, with aprons made out of feed sacks for both Kryssy and me. This was my very first Christmas gift. The Kulkowskis were good to us too, and we had money of our own. I knew then it was good we had left Kentucky, and here we were with friends in three states of this big new country.

After Mrs. Kulkowski got better, I got another job in a desk factory at thirty-five dollars a week. Stephan's salary was raised, too, and soon we were saving money as well as paying for all our own needs, and most of our wants. However, more and more, our minds were turning toward Detroit. Sonya and Wladiek were planning on moving there, and they wrote us regularly from Kentucky telling us about it and wanting us to meet them there. They told us about some old friends from the German camp, the Muncheks, who had settled there. I wanted to see them. It seemed that Detroit, with its automotive industry, was a melting pot for displaced persons, and soon I could think of little else.

It was hard to think of leaving the Kulkowski home though. By this time we knew their children and other relatives, and felt a part of the family. One thing convinced me, however, that we should leave. Mr. Kulkowski's brother owned a tavern where many Polish and German people came to sip beer and visit and sing. Stephan began to frequent this place more and more. I was afraid he would end up the way he had in Germany—staying away for long periods of time, coming home drunk, and being mean to Kryssy and me. Once I went with him to the tavern at the Kulkowskis' invitation, and everyone treated me well. They made me a special drink they called a "highball" because I told them I didn't like beer. I thought it was like soda pop, and took a sip from a little straw. Patty laughed, and when I looked surprised, she said, "That is not for sipping!" Well, I found out what a tavern was that night, and what a highball was, and I didn't like either one. I never went again, but Stephan went all the time.

Soon I was begging my husband to take me to Detroit. Letters from the Muncheks assured him he could make more money in the foundries there. Money meant a great deal to us at that time, and that was what convinced him finally to decide to leave. Secretly, I was hoping it would put an end to his drinking.

The Kulkowskis were so sad when we told them we were leaving that we decided to depart quickly. John drove us to the bus station the next week, leaving Patty home in tears. I called her from the station, "I'll come back to see you, and I'll write to you often, Ma," I promised. When we got to Chicago, I called her again. She was still choked up and couldn't talk. Again I said, "Don't worry, I'll never forget you. I'll come to see you again soon."

Truly we were leaving our family, and we loved them dearly. We had lived with them five months, and it was now 1951. But we anticipated a whole new and exciting life in Detroit. Little did I know the radical changes that would be made in my life in Michigan. I was still doing all the choosing. For so long people had told me every move to make, that I was rejoicing in my new freedom to direct my own life. I had never heard of Proverbs 3:6, or if I had, it had been so many years ago when I was a child that I had forgotten it. *I* was not acknowledging God, and He was not directing *my* paths—at least not in a way *I* could see. *I* had chosen to marry Stephan. *I* had chosen to come to the United States. *I* had chosen to sojourn in Wisconsin, and now *I* had chosen to move to Michigan, all because *I* wanted to.

17

Detroit—Fulfillment and Failure

✻

"...one's life does not consist in the abundance of the things he possesses" (Luke 12:15).

We were met in Detroit by our friends the Muncheks in the spring of 1951. They took us to their home until we could find jobs and an apartment. It didn't take long; we were just two weeks in our friends' house. Stephan found a job in a foundry, and I found a one-room apartment for the three of us. It was our first home by ourselves, and we were excited and thrilled.

Mrs. Munchek was washing dishes for a restaurant in the Detroit area, and she asked the manager if there might be a job for me. I wanted to work, but I didn't want to leave Kryssy. The manager asked if I could speak English, and thanks to Ma Patty, I could. She hired me and let me bring Kryssy to work with me. I had a bag of toys for her, and she sat and played with them for as long as I told her to. The fields of Kentucky had been good training for her.

I was hired to wash dishes at seventy-five cents an hour and went by bus with Mrs. Munchek every day except Sunday. Soon I graduated to making relish plates and other foods, and the manager called me her "right arm." I was pleased to realize all my training in hard work was bringing its reward. But now I was making money and not feeling used. This American system seemed good to me.

When I found out I was pregnant again and told my boss, she was kind to me and let me work almost up to my delivery date. In the meantime, we had been writing to Sonya and Wladiek in Kentucky and were thrilled to learn they were finally moving to Detroit also. We decided to move back together into one home to conserve expenses and help each other with baby-sitting. By now, Sonya had two little boys and one girl. I had Kryssy and another soon to be born. We found a two-bedroom apartment and moved in. Each couple had a private bedroom, and we kept the children on the studio couch in the living room. We ate all our meals together, and Sonya and I got along perfectly.

Wladiek found work in the same foundry with Stephan. Transportation was their biggest problem, so Stephan bought an old black Nash, and Wladiek drove it. Finally Wladiek taught Stephan how to drive, but he was afraid to take his test for a license. He wanted to take his family to the beach on Sunday like other Americans, but everyone warned him about driving without a license. He finally got up enough courage to take the test, and when he passed, was pleased and surprised. This opened up a whole new area of freedom to us as a family.

Treats to eat were still a source of great pleasure to me, and I kept trying out new things. One Saturday I bought a big bag of peanuts in the shell, and ate them all that day. I got such a stomachache I thought I would die. I didn't die, but I did go to the hospital that night. My Lilly was born early Sunday morning, February 24, 1952, after a fifteen-mile race through Detroit in the old black Nash. It was Lilly's impending birth, not the peanuts, that had made my stomach hurt.

I quit work now that I had two babies to take care of. Keeping house was fun, but the apartment seemed small. I wanted a home of my own again, and Stephan wanted some land of his own. Surprisingly, between our jobs in Wisconsin and Michigan, we had saved enough for a down payment on a house. We looked a long time, and finally found a small house on a good-sized piece of swampy land for a price we could afford. A ninety-seven-year-old woman had lived and died there, and it needed a lot of remodeling. Stephan took this as a challenge. A bank lent us two thousand dollars, and we closed the deal. We said goodbye to Sonya and Wladiek and they helped us move. Now we were home owners—another new experience in this new land.

I called Ma Patty in Wisconsin and told her about Lilly and our new home. She was glad we were getting along so well. We planned a visit to Wisconsin as soon as we got our home more livable. That was to take some time.

First, Stephan started on the yard, which needed a lot of fill. He found he could borrow a truck and haul ashes and waste home from the foundry for a base. Soon the yard was no longer wet, but it was very dirty. We worked and saved, and both of us together got enough money to buy topsoil. I spread dirt and sowed grass seed while Stephan was at work. At night, he hauled more for me to work on the next day. How happy I was when the first bit of green began to show. I was like everyone else now—I had a yard.

Then we started the remodeling. First we had to jack the house up and put a new foundation under it. Stephan borrowed jacks from the foundry, and we watched for houses being torn down to make room for freeways, and got all the lumber we needed for the remodeling.

There was no electricity or plumbing in the house. I didn't think Stephan could put it in himself, but he bought books and learned. He started on the wiring, and it was a great day when the inspector came and pronounced it good enough to pass the code. We turned on our lights, and rejoiced.

The plumbing project was next. We put in a new bathroom and kitchen, making the old kitchen into a third bedroom. The Muncheks and Sonya and Wladiek worked right with us. What good friends they were!

With those projects finished, we bought lumber and built a garage. We spent what little savings were left on new siding for the whole house and garage. Our project was complete. We had worked together on the whole thing, and had had little time for anything else, but it had brought us closer together. We had borrowed little money because we did the work ourselves, and because of Stephan's resourcefulness. Now we were ready for a big purchase.

I had been over to the neighbors' more since our house project was finished, and I told Stephan, "I want to be like other Americans and not have our plumbing freeze up in the winter." (The first winter of our remodeling we had had that happen constantly.) He went with me to examine the neighbors' heating stove. They told us it was called a gas furnace. *Oh, how beautiful,* I thought, *but too wonderful for us.*

Stephan and I went to a store to buy a big wood heating stove. The ones we saw looked luxurious compared to the Kentucky stoves and the German camp stoves and the Russian *petch.* However, the more I visited my neighbors, the more I saw the value of the furnace—no wood and dirt, no ashes, no firing each day—and I kept begging Stephan.

He didn't want to talk about it, because it meant a big debt. But he finally gave in and went to see a furnace man. When the man promised to include the installation of the furnace in the price, Stephan gave in. I think he was getting tired of working day and night. We were ignorant of time installment procedures, and really got "taken," as the Americans said, on the purchase contract. But at least we were warm, and we didn't have sense enough to know we had been tricked.

At last, the house was as nice as, or nicer than, any on the block. I was so proud; I was like everybody else, finally. I looked American; I lived in an American house; I had the major living conveniences of an American home. Or at least that is how it appeared on the outside.

If you had stepped inside my home, you would have been surprised. We had only the bare necessities of furniture in the house—stove, sink, table and chairs on a bare floor in the kitchen; we slept on blankets on the floors in the bedrooms; and the living room was bare. I only let my visitors into my kitchen, and no one knew how little we had. However, we only owed two thousand dollars to the bank on the house, and the furnace bill. Then suddenly, things changed.

Maybe we were so proud of being like everyone else that we forgot our "old country" ways;—paying for everything as we went along, and working hard so that we had no bills was a way of life for us. Maybe we were getting too materialistic, having tasted what it was like to have money and the power to buy things. Whatever the cause, Stephan began to spend wildly. He bought carpet for the house, and new furniture—not much, but enough—and foolishly, he charged it all.

To top it all off, he brought home a brand-new, light-blue Chevrolet sedan. He paid eight hundred dollars too much for it, our neighbor said, but this didn't seem to bother him. He got another bank loan for it, and we were too excited to think of worrying about the price. The girls and I were thrilled with our new car. But the monthly payments were mounting up.

To add to the financial disaster, I became pregnant again. Ruthie was born on June 15, 1953, when Kryssy was five and Lilly was one. I thought I couldn't be happier—new home, new car, three lovely daughters, and a husband who worked hard and seemed to want to give us everything. My happiness glossed over my lack of peace with God that haunted me each time I saw a church or let my mind dwell on my lost family in Russia. I tried to forget Father's last words to me, but when I did think of them, I had no assurance whatever that I would meet him in heaven.

I hadn't gone to church since I was in Wisconsin. It hadn't been a very happy experience there. That might have been because I wasn't communicating in English very well then. The preaching was in English, but all I had was my Polish Bible. I'd just get one Bible reference looked up and start to read the verse, when the preacher would give another. I finally began to copy them down and look them up at home. The Kulkowskis went to another church and attended an early service, and since Stephan didn't go at all, if I went to my church, I had to go alone and miss all the happy family times. I just didn't have that kind of commitment to God, so I didn't go anymore.

Then when we got to Detroit, the house kept us so busy for so long, I got out of the habit completely and never even thought about going to church. But God was faithful to me, and through the crises of my life He pursued me. As C. S. Lewis wrote, "He whispered to me in my joy, and shouted to me in my pain." The next pain I was to feel would indeed cause me to listen to Him.

We went on our trip to Wisconsin to visit the Kulkowskis in our new blue Chevy, so I could keep my promise to Ma Patty. It was after we returned from that trip that things changed in our lives. Maybe it was worry over the mounting bills; perhaps it was the lack of a work project; perhaps it was my preoccupation with my home and three little girls; perhaps it was a combination of any or all. Whatever it was, I noticed that Stephan began to come home a little later each day from work. When I asked him about it, he just said, "I stopped for a beer with some of the boys."

This didn't worry me too much at first. I was busy with the new baby, the house, and gardening. It felt so good when people stopped and praised my flowers. I swelled with pride. For so long I had felt deprived and a prisoner of circumstance. Now I was free, and had everything. Everything? Then why did I feel so incomplete, so empty at times? What did I lack? I couldn't figure it out. I didn't know the happiness these things were bringing me was temporary. I didn't know either how easily I could lose them all.

18

Divorce—A Tearing Time

✳

Therefore a man shall leave his father and mother and be joined to his wife (Gen. 2:24).

It was 1953, and we had lived in Detroit for two years, when Stephan began spending so much time away from home. He was still kind to the children and me, but didn't seem to want to be with us. I became fearful when I smelled liquor on his breath each time he came home. He still was quiet and had not learned to converse well in English. I, on the other hand, was able to converse well and did so a great deal with friends and neighbors.

We argued most about money at first. I never saw any of his check, except for the ten dollars he would leave with me monthly to pay the milk bill. Since I had worked and enjoyed having spending money, I felt cheated. I felt it was unfair that I had to stay at home and do a hard day's work of housekeeping and child care, but never had any money for myself. I began to resent the money he spent on liquor.

Resentment led to scheming. When I paid the milk bill, I would keep out a dollar or some change and save it. When I got five dollars, I would take all three girls and walk to a shopping center and spend it all as I liked. This was my fun, and I looked forward to it and saved religiously toward it. I usually bought the girls little trinkets, or fabric to make clothes for them, and treats for us all. Somehow

Stephan began to notice the milk bills getting higher and higher, and made me buy milk at the grocery store instead. He took me to the store once a week and I bought what I needed. He paid the bill, but I had to make the food last. Stephan was not only staying away later each day, he was staying away from home weekends too. Many times I ran out of milk completely, and had to walk two miles to buy some, taking all three girls with me. The resentment in me was growing.

When Stephan did come home, it was just to sleep and eat. While he slept, I checked the car and found bottles of liquor in it. My fears were substantiated. What could I do? I felt the old feeling in the pit of my stomach so familiar in the last days at Wünsdorf.

I began to turn more and more to neighbors for companionship. I saw an advertisement in a neighbor's paper for a couch for five dollars. I had saved that much here and there, and I went to see it. The lady, Mrs. Hodgeson, didn't like to charge anything, she said, because it was in such bad shape. I didn't care what shape it was in, because Stephan had stopped buying furniture before getting anything for the living room, and I wanted a couch. So I bought it and Mrs. Hodgeson had her friend deliver it to me. That started a friendship between us.

She brought me boxes of things—knickknacks and the like—and encouraged me a lot. She had asked where my husband was, and I was ashamed to tell her. However, because she was kind and told me she was a Christian, I broke down and told her everything. I really needed to confide in someone I could trust, who did not know us well, so they could give me unbiased advice. Sonya and Wladiek were too close to both Stephan and me; and they and the Muncheks would not have thought there was anything wrong with Stephan's drinking.

I baby-sat for Mrs. Hodgeson and she told me one day

when I came that she was divorced. I wondered at that a little, since she had told me she was a Christian. In spite of my failure to live a Christian life myself, I still held rigidly to things my father had taught me. Because she was divorced, I didn't ask her about her church, but she told me about it anyway. She went to a large church in Hazel Park, she said, and she told me she thought I would enjoy it. I guess I was waiting for someone to invite me to a church, and when she did, I went the very next Sunday. I found there were people in my neighborhood who went to that church and would give me a ride each Sunday. On Monday morning after I had attended on Sunday, an elderly couple from the church called at my home. I was surprised and pleased. These people were kind, and seemed like a mother and a father to me. They told me their ministry was to call on all those who filled out a visitor's card on a Sunday morning. That really impressed me. The church was beautiful, the people were beautiful, and I loved to go.

Again I took my Bible to church and wrote down all the references in the pastor's message to look up when I got home. I began to feel closer to God again as I went regularly to His house. The girls enjoyed the Sunday school. Some of what the pastor preached began to make sense to me. He talked about repentance—being sorry for your sins—conversion—turning from your sin and becoming a "new creature in Christ Jesus"—and commitment—making Christ Lord of your life and living for Him instead of for yourself. I began to think seriously of all these things in relation to my own life.

Along with the salvation messages, I began to learn from the Bible about marriage and the home. Oh, how I wanted Stephan to come home and stay so we could enjoy each other! I tried to tell him that, but he acted as if I were finding fault with him. I wanted him to know I loved him, which I had grown to do through the years, but I didn't put it into words. I thought I could show him if only he would stay at home long enough.

The foundry where he worked began calling the neighbors for him. They would come over and get me to answer the phone and the shop foreman would ask me why Stephan wasn't at work. I hadn't even known he wasn't there, so the next time he came home, I asked him about it.

"I was fishing," he said.

"Why don't you take us with you?" I begged. "Then we can all be together." He only brushed me aside and left again.

All this time he was not going to work, of course, the bills were piling up. Phone calls and collectors began coming about them. I tried to ask Stephan why he drank and didn't go to work and didn't pay the bills. "Am I the reason you drink?" I questioned.

"No!" he shouted angrily. "What's wrong with drinking? My father drank, my uncles drank, my brother drank, and I drink. There is nothing wrong with it, so leave me alone." Again he stomped out of the door. It seemed I couldn't say anything right. This quiet man I had married was no longer quiet. When he drank he was loud and angry and boastful—and dangerous.

Once more in my life I began to become desperate for food. The people at the church quickly realized my condition and helped me a lot with food showers. I found a little grocery nearby which was higher-priced than the supermarket, but which would charge food to me and deliver it. I didn't realize their prices were higher. I just knew I needed food. I tried to charge as little as possible because I knew the bill would never be paid. As soon as it was too high, my credit would be cut off.

Because I constantly wondered, I asked Stephan where he stayed when he was away from home for the weekend.

He began to boast about the women he met in the taverns and how nice they were to him. "I stay with them," he said.

I was heartbroken. "How can you do this to me?" I cried. "Don't you know I am faithful to you?"

"Foolish woman," he jeered, "I love you; I am married to you. So what if I go out with other women? They mean nothing to me. It's just a little pleasure."

Our life went from bad to worse. The little girls began to be afraid of their father. Every time he came home there were quarrels and loud talking and boasts and threats. They began to run to me when he walked in the door. This made him angry. "What are you telling them about me?" he would shout, swinging his fist at me. The girls and I ran to the neighbor's. I had told the children nothing but that Daddy was working, or Daddy was fishing. However, four years had passed and both Kryssy and Lilly were in school. They heard what people said. They knew how the other children taunted them, and why. They understood much more than I thought they did.

The neighbors called the police many times in the next few months as Stephan became more and more abusive. It was the liquor that drove him to near-madness. I thanked God he didn't come home very often now. I began to wish I had died in Germany. At least there, I only had myself to worry about. There, only I suffered. Now I had three little girls who were suffering too.

My neighbors and friends told me I must divorce Stephan—that I couldn't let him come home anymore and hurt us. All I could think of was how good he had been in the past. I thought of the three little dolls that called him "Daddy." I really had learned to love him, and I prayed for a miracle.

Finances got so bad I had to look for work. A neighbor, Nancy Pacquin, whose children were all in college, adopted me, in a way. She took me to job interviews, and got me a book to study so I could pass my driver's test. All this was a helpful diversion in my sad life. She taught me to drive and took me to the police station to take my test. As I drove out of the station lot for my test drive, I sideswiped a parked car. Needless to say, I didn't pass the test, but the officer encouraged me to practice more and try again. "You're just nervous," he said. My friend wouldn't let me give up, and I finally did pass the test.

Two days before Christmas I was called to work. Another neighbor, Mrs. Hoffman, offered to babysit for me. *What would I do without her?* I thought. She was such a friend to the girls and me. Then I found out she drank, and I was afraid for my children. I bought pop for her, and begged her not to drink while my Kryssy, Lilly, and Ruthie were with her. She thought I was a little crazy, but in reality I was desperate—I had to work.

One day Stephan came home and asked me to help him. "I think I am in trouble," he said. "I am sick and in great pain, and need to see a doctor right away. Will you help me?"

Of course I would help him. *Maybe this will bring us together,* I thought to myself. I called the doctor and took Stephan to his appointment. He was very quiet. I waited in the reception room while the doctor examined him. I questioned him when he came out, but he would tell me nothing. We stopped at the drugstore on the way home to get his prescription filled.

I felt sorry for Stephan. He seemed so quiet and defeated when we got home, and he lay on the couch too weak and sick to leave. I told him he should stay at home and get well. I said, "I want to continue to be your wife, and I want you to be the girls' father. All the neighbors tell me to divorce you, Stephan, but you are my husband, and the father of my children, and I cannot." He seemed to appreciate my words, but also seemed to be in some kind of depression. He stayed at home, but kept entirely to himself, as much as our home would allow.

For a while things seemed to be working out, but as soon as Stephan started feeling better, he began to stay away from home again. We hardly ever saw him. When I answered a phone call for Stephan at the neighbor's, I said, "Stephan is not home. Who is this?"

"I am his wife," a woman replied sneeringly.

"His wife?" I cried. "Who are you trying to kid? I am Stephan's wife, and we have three daughters!"

The woman's voice was mocking as she replied, "You may think you are his wife, but I really am, and I have the papers to prove it."

It was the end. I could stand the loneliness, the nonsupport, the cruelty, the disgrace, but this—this was too much. My friends took me to file for divorce.

19

From This Day Forward

❋

Have mercy on me, O Lord, for I am in trouble;
My eye wastes away with grief (Ps. 31:9).

The lawyer talked to me, but I still wasn't convinced. He told me, "You must not let him in the house during this period of separation."

"How can I do that?" I asked. "He is my children's father."

"You must do it because it is the law," he replied firmly. I agreed half-heartedly, but I did not intend to keep Stephan away.

Meanwhile the bills were piling up. I put an advertisement in the newspaper to do ironing in people's homes. The girls could go with me, and it gave me a little extra money, as well as getting us away from the house some. The girls continued to go to church, but I was always too tired.

The situation got worse. The neighbors were angry at me because I wouldn't call the police when Stephan came around. On the other hand, Stephan was threatening to hurt me if I divorced him. Finally I went back to the lawyer at the end of the separation, and told him the truth about Stephan's frequent visits. He was very angry and asked, "Why do you come to me if you're not going to do what I tell you?"

I cried, "He's my husband, don't you understand, and my children's father!"

"Your children will grow up to hate you if you keep on like this," he retorted. I got angry and walked out.

I thought things couldn't get any worse, but they did. I began to try to keep Stephan out. He threatened me, and my stomach ulcers began to give me trouble. I vomited blood regularly. Every day was filled with pain and fear. I was at the end of my rope. I had to go back to the lawyer and promise him anything to get some help and some peace of mind.

On the day the divorce was granted, I told Stephan in court, "I wish you would be our husband and father again." He was totally unmoved. I didn't see him again for a long time.

It had been almost a year since the separation and divorce proceedings had been started. It was fall again, and the girls went off to school. Only Ruthie needed a babysitter. My health had improved somewhat, and my friend, Norma, who had taken me to the lawyer, told me about a plastics factory that was hiring. The pay was good. She was going to apply there, and she wanted me to. I really wanted to, because even though I had been awarded the house and the car after the divorce, the expenses for the four of us never seemed to be completely covered by my small salary.

I got a job, and so did Norma. Starting a new job, however, caused me to start other new things. I rode to work with Norma, and, every Friday, she, along with most of the other girls from the factory, stopped at a bar to cash her check. That meant I had to stop, too, though I worried about my little ones at home alone. Ruthie was cared for by a neighbor during the day, but when Kryssy came home from school, she picked up her little sister and took her home. I got home soon after they did.

I never drank, for I hated liquor more than ever since my break with Stephan. But at the bar I found fellowship and friends. The girls would tease me and suggest I was too young and pretty to bury myself because of a problem with one man. "There are lots of fish in the sea," they said, "you are free now. Life is just beginning for you!"

"I will never let another man touch me," I solemnly vowed.

They laughed, "You'll change your mind when the right one comes along."

And change I did, stubbornly and haltingly, and more quickly than I ever dreamed.

A lot of people begin to look out in special ways for a young divorcée. Mrs. Hoffman, my babysitter, was special to me in this way. All who were close to her called her Blondie because of her beautiful hair. I asked her where she had it cut and styled, and she told me, "At Helen Kauppila's." Then she added enthusiastically, "Why don't you do it too?" It was a few days before Christmas, and I thought that was a great idea.

Blondie took me to Helen's home, where she did hair styling. She had a sick husband, and a son in the Air Force. We went to her house early on a Saturday morning and I left my children sleeping. I hoped to be back home with them before noon. I was excited at the thought of having a haircut and a permanent. It was a first for me.

Helen seemed quite glad to meet me, and so did her husband, who was home from the Veterans' hospital for a few days over the holidays. Blondie must have told them about me, for they were very friendly. However, they weren't the kind of people I would have chosen for my friends, I thought. There were beer bottles strewn throughout the kitchen, and both Helen and Blondie were chain smokers. All three were using profane language such as I had never heard before in a home. Nevertheless, I tried to be friendly for Blondie's sake. She had been so good to me, I didn't want to hurt her friends.

Some time passed and no one made any move to do my hair. I was concerned about getting home to the girls, so I asked when we could start. "As soon as we get Sleeping Beauty out of the room," Helen replied smilingly.

Dick, her husband, shouted, "Get him up then!" Helen went to the door off the kitchen and hollered at the unknown person. I couldn't figure out what was going on, but I soon learned.

Helen turned to me: "Why are you in such a hurry? You are a single girl, and you know you want to get married. I've got just the man for you—my handsome, intelligent son is here, and you are in such a hurry, you may not get to meet him."

Just then the "handsome" young man came stumbling out of the lounge/shop room where he had been sleeping. I took one look at him and turned to Helen, saying, "I need to get home to my kids!"

"O.K., O.K.," she answered irritably. "Let's get on with you." I went on into the shop with her, and it didn't seem too long until my hair was done. All the while I could hear the merriment in the kitchen. Handsome Son must have been a favorite of Blondie's too.

When my hair was done, I sat in the living room while Helen worked on Blondie. I had just put my head down to rest when Handsome Son came strolling in. "Hi," he said, "my name is Roy." He flipped some dials on the radio and music filled the room. "Do you like it?" he asked.

"It's O.K.," I answered unenthusiastically.

"You're not very sociable are you?" he teased. I didn't answer. "What would you like? A drink? A dance?" he continued. I shook my head. "What a bore!" he said laughingly. "My mother and father like you, but I don't."

"That's good," I retorted, "because I don't like you

either. I'm not interested in men, and I haven't met a good one yet except for my father." My bitterness was very evident as I stood up and walked out into the kitchen. Helen was still working on Blondie in the shop.

Roy followed me out into the kitchen where his father was and asked gently, "Do you want a beer? No? Well, pop then?" All I did was shake my head to everything he said. What I really wanted was to be left alone. He changed his approach then. "I've heard about you," he said, "you've been badly hurt, but you need a friend. Come, let me take you down the street and get you some pop." I was tired of waiting, and welcomed anything to help pass time right then, so I walked down the street with him. He led me to an open door. I stopped abruptly—it was a tavern. Roy took me by the arm, "They have pop here," he said, "just sit with me here and have a pop while I have a beer." I didn't want to make a scene, so I sat down and drank my pop quickly. Roy wasn't done with his beer when I rose to go. He grimaced and paid the bill and followed me out.

Blondie was ready when I got back, and we left quickly. I didn't like those people at all. I might have needed a friend, but I was convinced it was not Roy Kauppila.

The girls were all awake when I got home, and we started on our Saturday work. Blondie came over and got me for a phone call in midafternoon. It was Roy. His voice was gentle and kind over the phone. "You are a great person, but you need a friend. Would you like a friend to come and visit you?"

I said "No!" emphatically, but he kept insisting. "It's a holiday, remember?"

"I don't care what day it is," I answered. "I don't want any man around here. I have to take care of my children." I hung up abruptly and thought I was rid of him for good.

An hour later he was knocking on my door. "I took a bus over to bring you a present," he said smilingly, holding up an assortment of soft drinks in a carton. "See, I don't even have any beer. Can I come in?" Deep in my heart I appreciated his gift, and I always had trouble being deliberately discourteous, so I let him in. He looked at the three little faces staring at him from the other doorway. "You need lots of mending here," he said, nodding at the girls, "Can I help?"

"I don't want your help," I replied. "I'm not interested in men, I told you."

"I hear many people say that," he said, "but they change their minds." He was gentlemanly, and stayed just a little while, but I was relieved when he left.

He came back again in two days. "It's Christmas," he explained, "and I haven't been home in eight years. I only came home because my father is ill. I don't know many people, and I'll be gone again in a few days. Let's be friends." I didn't have the heart to refuse that argument. I felt sorry for him and his family. The longing for my own family filled me with pity.

Roy came every day through the holiday season when I was not working. I looked forward to the day he would go back to the Air Force, because his presence was beginning to disturb me—my defenses were breaking down. He was so nice to me, so gentle, so good to the girls. They began to look forward to his coming.

Roy told me one night he was leaving soon and asked to see me one more time. I wasn't enthusiastic, but when he called me at work and asked me to drive him to the bus station, I agreed. I thought, *After this, he will be gone for good. What can it hurt?* He was very handsome in his uniform, and laughed when I gave him two quarts of my homemade dill pickles as a farewell gift. Then he was gone on the bus to North Carolina, leaving behind a lonely woman with a promise of a letter.

He did write—every day for two months—and he called

every week. "I like you, Tania," he said, "and I don't care who knows it!" My bruised ego and broken, lonely heart began to respond. Toward the end of February he called more often, and one night on the phone he said, "Tania, I want you to marry me. Even if you cannot love me, it would be enough to have you live with me and be the mother of my children. You are such a good mother, and I have never had such a home." I weakened more at those pleas.

Roy came home on furlough in March, and I met him at the airport. I hadn't driven more than a few feet away from the airport with him into the countryside, when he told me to pull over. I obeyed and he took my left hand and put a ring on the third finger. "If you like me at all and will marry me," he said, "kiss me!" I leaned over and kissed him on the cheek. "Do you call that a kiss?" he asked laughingly, but he demanded no more, and we set our wedding date.

On March 21, 1959, I became Mrs. Roy Kauppila in Roy's church. All my resolve to be done with men for life had melted away. My three little girls were all dressed in light blue like their mommy and watched happily from the pew. Roy had told them, "I am marrying you three, too," and indeed he was. Once again I was starting a new life. *Will my happiness last this time?* my heart seemed to cry within my breast. It had been crying so loudly, and for so long, that I was deaf to the still, small voice of God. He would have to shout at me, too.

20

A New Tania

❋

Therefore, if anyone is in Christ, he is a new creation; old things have passed away; behold, all things have become new (2 Cor. 5:17).

After the wedding ceremony and a potluck reception at the church, which Roy's mother arranged, we stopped at home. Mrs. Hoffman was going to stay right at the house with the girls, while I went on a week's honeymoon. The goodbyes were tearful. I wasn't sure I wanted to be married, or go on a honeymoon if it meant leaving my children. But everyone urged me on and assured me everything would be all right, and we went.

We stopped in Chicago and then went on to Wisconsin, where I introduced Roy to Patty and John. They were surprised that I had remarried. My letters of the divorce and preceding difficulties had been so bitter, that they thought I would never marry again. I hadn't written them about Roy because it had all happened so fast.

When we stopped for meals, Roy would have a beer with his meal, but no more. He was trying to please me, and I was grateful. But in my mind a gnawing fear kept cropping up—*Did I do right to marry?*

We went up to the Upper Peninsula of Michigan to visit some of Roy's relatives, and my fear materialized. Roy bought a case of beer to drink and celebrate with his family, and he consumed it all that evening. The next day he bought another—some special kind found only in the Upper Peninsula—to take home to Mrs. Hoffman for babysitting. It was all gone before we reached Detroit.

I had called home that morning and found out the three girls were sick from loneliness. "It is good you are coming home, Tania," Mrs. Hoffman told me.

I almost forgot about Roy's drinking in my anxiety to get home. When we got there only Kryssy was still sick in bed, but all three looked weak and pale. "Lord, did I do the right thing?" I prayed.

There was a Kauppila reunion soon after we got home, and again, Roy drank too much. "Did I do right to marry you, Roy?" I asked him on the way home.

"We're all right," he answered drunkenly, "just don't argue about drinking. There is nothing wrong with having a few drinks."

I went back to work, and Roy worked on the official details of getting a discharge from the service while he baby-sat for me. Before, he had wanted to be in the Air Force; now he wanted out. They would let him out, but he would have to report back to his base first.

I took him to the airport, but we didn't talk. There was a barrier between us. I was obsessed with the idea that I had made a wrong choice. I couldn't talk or pray about it. I was back to my childhood belief that God could not exist and allow people to be so miserable. I was as unhappy as I had ever been in Russia or the concentration camp, but in a different way. I was still a prisoner, but in a prison of my own making.

After Roy boarded the plane, I ran to the car and rolled up all the windows, locked the doors, and collapsed. I thought I would die, my chest hurt so badly. It was as if a dam broke when the tears came. I cried so hard, and then I must have fainted, for the next thing I remember is seeing the airport parking attendant peering in through the

closed window. "Are you O.K., lady?" he asked, his fore-
head wrinkled with concern. I nodded weakly, affirmatively.
After he left, I fell into my old pattern of praying in spite of
my professed unbelief. "If you are there, God, do something so I never have to see Roy again—so I never have to
go through another broken marriage."

Roy was gone a month, and I was in control of myself
again by the time he came home, discharged from the Air
Force. He started looking for a job immediately, but he
couldn't find one very easily, and I continued working.
When he did find a job, he didn't work at it long. Beer was
always in the house. Often he didn't finish one bottle
before he'd open another. I thought he must be crazy to
do that—that his mind was affected. Roy just laughed at
me. "You'd understand if you drank!" he said.

I wondered how he could have been so sincere before
we were married, and change so quickly. We had been
married only a few weeks and we were already separated
in spirit. He hadn't found a steady job in that time either. I
just went on numbly from day to day. I was sad—I felt I
had failed again. Now I alternated between thinking there
was no God, and blaming Him for all my troubles.

Roy started staying away for two and three weeks at a
time. My imagination ran wild. I called everywhere to try to
locate him. I went to bars and brought him home. Whenever he was sober, he would assure me I was the only
woman he ever had loved. Sometimes Roy honestly tried
to stop drinking, and I would hope again that our marriage
could be happy. Then just one drink would begin the
nightmare all over again. This was to become our pattern
in those early years: Roy was a tender, loving husband
when sober, but an entirely different man when he was
not.

The strain began to take its toll on my health again. I got
thinner and thinner, and my ulcers bled constantly. I got

so weak I could scarcely work. What a terrible time for my children. *Two men, one after the other, have robbed them of their happiness,* I thought.

One Friday I couldn't get out of bed. When Roy saw how sick I was, he stayed around to take care of the girls. On Sunday morning I was too weak to open my eyes or lift my head. I still didn't want to go to the hospital, but Roy carried me to the car and drove me there. In the emergency room, they admitted me for immediate surgery. The diagnosis was severe internal hemorrhaging.

After the surgery, the doctors told Roy, "She's not going to make it." Roy rushed out and didn't return. He felt sorry for himself and guilty. My life hung in the balance in that intensive care room for a week. The medical staff tried transfusions, but my body rejected them. I knew nothing. Then one night I remember seeing a square of white above me, with four sides. My mind tried to place where I was, but I was so tired that I lapsed into unconsciousness again.

The next day I saw black specks moving back and forth in the white square. As my eyes focused on doctors and nurses and the ceiling of the hospital room, I knew where I was. As soon as I could talk, I found out how long I had been there and made arrangements to have someone call my home and check on the children. They had been alone, the neighbors helping to care for them, but no one knew where I had gone. Roy had never gone home. He didn't notify my boss at work or neighbors at home. They had even begun to wonder if I had died.

Died! I thought. *What if I had died? Where would I be now?* "Oh, Papa," I cried, "I wouldn't have met you in heaven if I had died." I knew I was not a Christian; no matter how many times I had joined churches; no matter how many times I had been baptized; no matter that I had attended a catechism class; even though my parents were

Christians, I was not a part of God's family, nor walking in His way.

God brought to my mind a puzzle Lilly had brought home from Sunday school a few weeks earlier. I had tried to help her figure it out, but I couldn't. We had to wait for the answer from the teacher the next week. The puzzle was this: If you were alone in a room and on each side of you was a wall—one of brick, one of sea, one of fire, and one of darkness—how would you get out of that room? God spoke to my heart: "You are that person all shut in with many walls. Light your life with My consuming fire, and I will show you the way out through the darkness of your life."

I began to cry out to God. I told Him what a sinner I was to lie and act selfishly; to reject His existence and go my own way; to expect my husband to change and not change myself; to compromise in my lifestyle from what I knew to be right; to disobey God's Word in so many ways; to be a hypocrite and think I was better than others because of what I didn't do. I thanked Him for sparing my life, and told Him if He wanted to take it right then, I would trust Him with it and with the lives of my children who would be left behind alone. But I promised that every day He chose to give me life, I would glorify Him with each breath I took. All my guilt and bitterness, shame and fear, lostness and hopelessness, rolled off me like a heavy peddler's sack put down. I was happy and peaceful for the first time in my whole life. I knew I was a child of God. No one had to tell me—the Holy Spirit witnessed within me. I was different and I knew it. The words I had heard in church about repentance and commitment finally made sense to me. God Himself had led me through each step of conversion—repentance, confession, faith, commitment, assurance, and thanksgiving. I was changed in a moment.

Before this happened, I had made scene after scene in

the hall and my room, crying and screaming in depression because Roy did not come; because my children were home alone; because I thought I had lost my job; because I was weak and sick and didn't want to face reality. Now, all the doctors and nurses, who before had quieted me with hypodermics to make me sleep, marveled at the new quiet, calm Tania.

When I got strong enough, I called the church I had attended before I met Roy and where my children had been going to Sunday school. "We just heard what happened to you, Mrs. Kauppila," they said. "We have been trying to find out for several days, and we have been praying for you." They prayed and they visited, both at my home and at the hospital. They sent cards and flowers and fruit. They brought me an English Bible, books, and tracts to read. They had come before, but hadn't been allowed in my room because I was so sick and distraught. I remembered then all the times I had seen people coming up to the door of my house and had locked it and had hidden in the bedroom so I wouldn't have to face them. Now everything was different. I was a new person in Christ Jesus, and nothing in life could ever touch me again except by the direct will of the God of heaven.

This God would show me how powerful He was in many ways in the year to come. But for now, it was enough that my life had been spared and my soul had been given new life in Jesus, so that I would never die.

21

Miracles

Now to Him who is able to do exceeding abundantly above
all that we ask or think, ... to Him be glory in the church by
Christ Jesus throughout all ages, world without end. Amen
(Eph. 3:20–21).

After my conversion, it seemed even my physical strength
was renewed. I came back from death's door quickly, and
God gave me another extension on my life. Soon, I was
ready to go home from the hospital and convalesce. I
called a few friends the day the doctor told me I could go
home, but none of them were home. Finally, I called one
of the families from the church and asked them to bring
my girls to the hospital so I could see them and go home
with them.

The girls were brought, but there was so much red tape
connected with my discharge that it wasn't until late
afternoon I finally could leave with my three little ones.
They had waited all day with me. By that time I had gotten
hold of Blondie, and her husband came and got the four
of us. What a homecoming it was. We were all talking at
once and hugging and kissing. I was still weak, and trying
to move with three little girls hanging on me was ridiculous.

When I got home, my mother-in-law came over to help
me get settled. While she was there Roy came home, too. I
heard his voice in the kitchen, and I heard his mother say
to him, "You be good to her; take care of her; this is your
home, your wife, your children."

Roy had been home with us for a week when I found out he had lost his job, his car, and everything he had. God kept me from saying things I shouldn't that week. I knew right then that God had changed me, because the old Tania would never have been able to keep quiet. When Roy would ask me if he could do anything for me, I just answered, "No thanks, honey."

He stood silently beside me for a long time. "I don't blame you for not wanting my help," he said. "I don't work and support you. Besides that, I didn't come to see you in the hospital. But I ask you one more time, will you forgive me? I want to try again to keep at least one promise I made you when I married you."

I looked up into his face and said, "I've already forgiven you, honey."

He hugged me and questioned me: "How could you forgive me before I even asked?"

I rested in his arms and told him, "My father taught me many years ago, that if you want God to forgive you, you must forgive everyone else in the very same way you want Him to forgive you."

Roy looked surprised. "But you weren't always like this; how are you able to forgive me now, after the way I've treated you?"

Then I told him everything that had happened to me in the hospital—how I had almost died; how I felt all boxed in in our life and couldn't find any way out of our circumstances. I said, "Honey, God showed me the way out. I saw myself a sinner in need of forgiveness. I used to think you were the sinner, that I was good and you were bad, but God lit my way through that dark wall and I could see. I could see we were both the same—helpless sinners. I really felt I deserved to die then, and where I had been afraid of death and eternity, afraid of leaving my girls, now I had peace that the God who was calling me to admit my sinfulness would take care of me in this life and the next. I cried out to Him, and He forgave me all my sin. He made a new Tania, and I promised Him I'd serve Him and give Him glory with every breath He allowed me, for each day He gave me life. So that's how I got this way. If God forgave me and received me as His brand-new child, do you think I could refuse to forgive anyone else, most of all you whom I love?"

By that time there were tears in Roy's eyes and he simply asked, "Tania, can we go to church together next Sunday?" When he said that, my heart condemned me. I had thought Roy would not want to go, so I had never asked him to go to my church with me. How could I have known what I knew as a child, been spared through so many trials in life, been as loving and intimate with another human being as I had with Roy, and never talk with him of God—never invite him to go to church with me? But thank God, He was greater than my heart, and from somewhere in the back of my mind there came the remembrance of a Scripture verse. "There is therefore now no condemnation to those who are in Christ Jesus" (Rom. 8:1). I could leave the failures of the past, and smile confidently at my husband, and agree to go to church with him the next Sunday.

The next Sunday I was sick, Roy had wrecked my car, it was too far to walk to church, and we had no money for bus or taxi. We could have called some of the church members we knew, and asked them to pick us up, but if I wasn't able to go, I didn't think Roy would want to go with strangers. Oh, how my mind tried to reason out life, when God had such a simple answer. When He is moving, there is power. When He is drawing men to Himself, there is no obstacle too great to get over. So when I thought Satan would win that Sunday, God worked a simple miracle. Roy made me comfortable on the couch and kissed me, and when the Sunday school bus came for our girls, he climbed on as well. So much for pride, when the Spirit of the Lord is working.

While at first my strength seemed to come back quickly, I wasn't able to work as I had before. A few hours of housework a day would tire me, and I would have to spend the rest of the day on the couch. But I had time to read and pray—and I did. I didn't know how to pray for Roy specifically, but I prayed hour after hour, and God heard and answered with just what Roy needed. "Delight yourself also in the LORD, and He shall give you the desires of your heart" (Ps. 37:4) became my special verse.

A few weeks later, on a Sunday, I was lying down resting, waiting for Roy and the girls to come home from church. Roy hadn't missed a Sunday since that first one, even though I had not been well enough to go. The day before I had spent a lot of energy cleaning up the house. Because of the labor camp, cleanliness had become an obsession with me. As I gazed happily at my shining floor, the door burst open, and Roy ran across the room, not stopping to take off his shoes, which was the rule of our house. "The message this morning was just for me, honey. You have a new husband, and the girls have a new father," he cried as he hugged me and then stood, looking down at me. He was so handsome standing there with his new smile. It was a few days before he explained it all to me, but I knew God had done something special for Roy.

The people from the church came to visit us—the same people who months before I had allowed to stand outside my door while I pretended not to be home. Now they taught us gently from the Bible what it meant to be Christians and to have a Christian home. Roy and I devoured every word, and couldn't wait to put it into practice. He eventually told me all about that Sunday when God gave him his new smile. He had gone forward in the church service that day to receive Christ. He had wanted to from the very first Sunday, but he was under such conviction that he just got more and more quiet. I was prepared for the worst, thinking his quietness might be a mood and a prelude to his leaving again. But I kept quiet, and God gave me the best. He redeemed Roy that Sunday, and our marriage, and the next months were heaven on earth. Truly God worked a miracle in saving both my husband and me.

The church was good to us. They never made me feel unworthy or ashamed because I was divorced and remarried. But it bothered me. I still had problems with Stephan, too. I had been afraid to tell Roy all the details before he became a Christian, for fear there would be a fight. Now I just prayed that God would work another miracle—and He did.

First, Roy started reading the Bible and praying with the family after our evening meal. I could hardly believe it was the same man who had been so alienated from me, now taking the Christian leadership in our home. Then one day he prayed for Stephan. I couldn't help it—the tears came. He prayed so lovingly for God to forgive my former husband and save him, and restore him to health and happiness. Thinking of the miracle in Roy that had brought him to this place helped me believe God could do the same for Stephan, and it helped me be more open with Roy about Stephan too.

I am still hoping for that miracle. God gave me the chance to visit Stephan in the hospital after he had been badly burned. When we heard about his accident, we took the girls to see him in the hospital, and we waited in the lobby. One day they came down and said, "Dad wants to see you, Mom." I thought, *I can't go, I don't want to see him.* Roy nodded his approval and the girls kept begging. Immediately I knew my thoughts were wrong. God's Spirit was faithful to His new child. I took my Polish Bible and went up to that hospital room, and when I saw how badly he was burned, I wept.

"Stephan," I cried, "forgive me for the way I treated you. I was trying to pay you back, and I'm sorry." There were tears in his eyes as he listened to me tell what God had done for me and Roy, but he didn't say anything. I explained lovingly the way he could find purpose in life through Jesus Christ, and we prayed together. I left then, and I have not seen him since. I pray that God began a miracle that day, and that Stephan has peace with God now. However, God did work another miracle that day, for me. He took from my mind the feeling that I had ever had any other husband than Roy. All the guilt of my wrong choices rolled off me as my dear husband led me to pray for Stephan. Now I think of my marriage to Roy as my only marriage—of Roy as my first and only husband.

We started having Bible studies right in our home. A young missionary and his wife on homeland furlough were serving as assistants to the pastor in our church. They led the studies in Ephesians. Other couples came too, and we grew in the Lord. We had much to learn. When we got to the fifth chapter, Roy learned how to love as a Christian husband should, and I learned how to submit as a Christian wife should.

One of the first things Roy asked me to do was to quit my job and stay home for good. That meant trusting him to support the family. That was a hard thing for me to do, because Roy's lifestyle up to then had been against us. But God brought the old refrain to my mind: "Trust and obey, for there's no other way." I fell on my knees right there in my familiar kitchen, and trusted God for our life. Roy needed to support us, and he needed to feel my trust. He got a job, and he did support the family. I happily stayed home.

I began to pray that God would allow me to share the joy He had given when He saved Roy and me. We invited Sonya's daughter, who was about Krys's age, to spend a week in our home during a school vacation. As she listened to Roy read the Bible and lead in prayer that week, she questioned us, and decided she wanted to be saved. When Sonya saw the difference in her life, I was able to lead her to the Lord. My very dear friend Sonya! How happy that has made me, to know that after all the hard times we have shared in the labor camp, and then in the Kentucky tobacco fields, that one day we will also share something much more wonderful: an eternity together in heaven with our blessed Lord.

Then one day when Mrs. Munchek visited in our home, I had the joy of leading her to the Lord when she was already seventy-two years old. Such a miracle of grace! How it warmed my heart.

Roy's mom and dad became two more miracles of God's grace. Mom was sick with cancer, and Roy and I witnessed to her day after day. She also saw the great change that had taken place in our lives. In the end, the pastor from our church prayed with her, and then Mom lifted her hand toward heaven before she died. Even though she was too weak to talk, we all believe she reached out to God that day in faith.

Even though Dad had been sick for years, he outlived Mom. During that time, he too accepted Christ as Savior, and the pastor told about it at his funeral. I could hardly believe what God was doing. The lifelong desires of my heart were being granted. And there was still more He was going to do. Before that, however, I had more spiritual lessons to learn.

22

The Lion Roars

> ...the devil walks about like a roaring lion, seeking whom he may devour (1 Pet. 5:8).

The miracles in our lives were not accomplished easily. Let me tell you how the "lion" roared and attacked us, trying to frighten us into discouragement and inactivity.

When the Lord saved Roy and me, we became new persons, with new desires. We loved going to our church, and being with other Christians. And Roy had a real zeal for serving the Lord, however he could do it. Since he had first gone to church on the Sunday school bus, he realized the potential of a bus ministry. Soon he was driving one of the buses on Sunday morning, and his route enlarged until he was picking up between fifty and sixty-five children each week. He loved the children.

Then he became involved in the teacher training class, so he could teach a class of young boys. His vision was to reach youngsters at an early age, before they began a life that would lead to one of heartache, such as his had been.

We were both encouraged to begin making house-to-house visitation calls, to invite people to come to church, especially those who did not attend church elsewhere. The first night we went, another couple took us with them; Roy went with the husband, and I with the wife. The Lord provided special miracles just for us: In the home in which the men called, a husband was saved; in the home in which we called, a husband, wife, and son were saved. We were jubilant! There is nothing like the special joy of winning someone to the Lord!

Roy was also working with young boys in the Christian Service Brigade at church one night a week. In addition, we were having a weekly Bible study in our home, conducted by one of the couples from church. Another night of the week we attended a Bible study at someone else's home. We really loved the fellowship and were learning so much about the Christian life.

Seven days and nights were now completely full for Roy—every day at his mill job, and every evening with regular church services, Bible studies, or service projects. We were such new Christians we didn't realize we should reserve some time for family life, or just to rest.

Then it happened. The "lion" began his roaring, as we became exhausted with activity. Roy came home from work one day, ill. Surgery for a double hernia was followed by a layoff from his job. He spent his recuperation time thinking about his "new life in Christ." Perhaps we had both gotten into too many things too quickly, but at any rate, Roy was convinced he was on some kind of merry-go-round. It was a burden, rather than a joy, especially while he was weak and sick. He wondered why God had allowed him to be sick, when he was holding down the first steady job of his life. He hadn't yet studied about Job and all his testings, and he didn't know why he was feeling so depressed. Ashamed to tell anyone his thoughts for fear they would think him a "poor testimony," he bore his depression alone, not even sharing these feelings with me.

We had been so close and our fellowship so sweet since we had become one in Christ, that I didn't want to question Roy when I thought I smelled liquor on his breath. I prayed for him and trusted him. But soon I knew that things weren't right. We weren't sharing Christ as we had before. I thought it was the illness and remained optimistic for a while.

After Roy was well, he didn't go back to work or to church, and started staying away from home again. When we would talk about it, Roy would say, "I'm still saved. There's nowhere in the Bible it says you have to go to church to be a Christian. There's nowhere it says you can't take a drink." But his eyes were filled with misery, and it seemed that to be home and to look at his wife and three daughters only made him more unhappy. He was consumed with guilt. Instead of confessing, he only drank more to forget, and his absences grew longer.

He finally left home for good after three or four months of backsliding. We were financially desperate and I had to admit to myself that the girls and I were on our own again. I went to the factory and got my old job back. Some of my friends at the church began urging me to carry through the divorce I had started before Roy was saved. They were kind and good to me, but very wrong in their advice. I loved Roy. We had grown so close in our short period of Christian marriage, that I felt I couldn't let him slip away from me.

When he occasionally called home he would say, "Hi, honey!" That encouraged me.

"Am I still your honey?" I would ask.

"Yes," he always answered, "I have no other, only you!"

"Come home, Roy," I begged. Once he did come home for a little while after a phone call such as that. He took me to another church nearby. I think he was ashamed to go back to our church. My hopes sky-rocketed, but the new resolutions didn't last long.

Roy's mother was still alive during this time, and had moved from the city to a big strawberry farm. She hired Roy by the day, and he worked long enough to get money for liquor, and then went off on a binge. One day I went to talk to him among the strawberry plants. He was rough and final. "It will never work with us," he said, "go home and forget me. We'll never make it. Every time I look at you it reminds me of how rotten I am." I went home, discouraged at last, hope gone.

Our Christian friends continued to say I was foolish and urged me to divorce him. I resisted, but there seemed no way out of the walled room again. I had never heard of Annie Johnson Flint then, but her God was my God. Like her, when I got to the "end of my hoarded resources, my Father's full giving had only begun."

One day in June I started two weeks' vacation from the factory. I couldn't understand why I felt so happy that first morning off work. I hadn't seen Roy for months, nor looked for him. But today there was a strange moving in my heart to look one last time. I didn't dare tell any of my friends. Besides, it was very early in the morning—the children were still sleeping. I woke Krys and told her to take care of the little ones and stay in the house until I came home. I went out in the semidarkness to start the car with no idea in what direction to start driving. I leaned my head on the steering wheel and prayed for God to lead me. Then I backed out of the driveway and headed north. I drove with no thought of destination. In fact, my thoughts were filled with a review of my life.

A short time later I found myself on an unfamiliar stretch of country road near Utica. "What am I doing here?" I wondered aloud. I saw a house across a field from which men were emerging to go to work in the fields, and I thought I would ask for information about Roy there. As I drove up in front of the house, God worked another miracle just for me: Roy stepped out of the house, shoes in hand, headed for the fields. He covered his surprise at seeing me there by treating me cruelly, as he had in the past. "What are you doing here?" he asked roughly.

"I just wanted to see you, to talk with you," I answered joyfully. I knew God was going to work a miracle in his heart. "Give me a hug and a kiss, honey," I teased.

"Yeah," he retorted sarcastically, but the miracle of my finding him on that remote farm in the early morning stopped him from walking away. He got in the car instead. "Now tell me, how did you find me?" he muttered.

With a smile I said, "I didn't, Roy, God did. He's known where you were all the time. I prayed God would let me find you just one more time to let me tell you again how much I love you, and He did." I leaned over and kissed him on the cheek. "Doesn't that remind you of our first kiss?" I asked tenderly.

He took me in his arms, and then pulled away and put his head down on the dash and cried. "How can I go home with you, looking like this, so dirty? I can't let the girls see me this way."

I put my arm around his shaking shoulders. "They will be glad to see you any way you come!"

"Glad to see you, Dad!" were the first words Roy heard as he entered our home that morning from three little girls all in pajamas, eyes heavy with sleep. We were a family again—back together for good, never to be parted again.

It was the first day of my vacation, and after we prayed and talked for a while, we decided to get away from Detroit for a few days and take a trip as a family. I had always wanted to go back to Wisconsin to see Ma Patty and John. They welcomed us like their lost family. When everyone else drank, Roy told them joyfully, "I quit drinking." His eyes met mine lovingly across the heads of people who didn't understand. We both knew Roy could never again take even one drink, and he never has. God miraculously delivered him from alcohol's power. We witnessed to the Kulkowskis about what God had done for us. They knew we were different.

When we got back to Detroit, Roy went back to the paper mill where he had worked before. He had lost his job because of absences and drinking, but his work record when he was sober was good, and when he reapplied giving his testimony and asking for another chance, God and the personnel manager gave it to him. I quit work again—this time with complete peace of mind and heart.

When I had had surgery, I had been told that, if I lived, I would never have any more children. God delights in proving Himself strong in the behalf of those whose hearts are right toward Him. And God had done so many impossible things for us that Roy and I had no fear in asking Him for a child, our child—the fruit of our renewed marriage. Did He give us one? No! He gave us two!

When we went to the doctor, the same one who had cared for me during my surgery, he asked me incredulously, "How did you get this way?" I knew what he meant, but I teasingly said, "Doctor, it is easy. Don't you know?" After we had a good laugh together, I explained what God had done for Roy and me, and he examined me and confirmed my pregnancy, shaking his head with wonder. Beautiful twin daughters, Tania and Nina, were born on February 19, 1963. Roy's joy was complete. But six women in the house made him work twice as hard.

Our next-door neighbor was a real estate agent, and he began to hire Roy to clean up and redecorate, in his spare time, the houses he was listing. This started Roy on a trade of his own. To catch up financially, he worked two jobs for a long time. But that didn't stop us from getting back to our church and becoming a part of it again. In his quiet way, Roy witnessed to what God had done for him, and the trials He had taken him through; from what he had been delivered, and to what he had been called. "I am a miracle of God's grace," he told the people of the church. Many tears washed people's faces that day, as the Holy Spirit convicted each of us and washed us clean of our own backslidings.

I never look at the sky on a clear night, without thinking of what God did for Roy and me and remembering the words of David the psalmist:

> When I consider Your heavens,
>   the work of Your fingers,
> The moon and the stars,
>   which You have ordained,
> What is man that You are mindful
>   of him...? (Ps. 8:3–4).

God had proved He was "mindful" of us!

23

In Fear and Trembling

And do not hide Your face from
  Your servant,
For I am in trouble;
Hear me speedily (Ps. 69:17).

The miracle of God's power in our lives went on and on,
through good times and bad. I wish I could tell you that we
came to a place in our lives where everything went smoothly.
It would make such an attractive, victorious ending to my
story, but it wasn't to be that way.

Again I was to fear for my life. Lessons I thought I had
learned well had to be relearned in other situations and
trials. I became sick, and there seemed to be no healing.
Even death became an unwelcome visitor to our home.
But over and over, God gave of His blessing to me, and
proved His promise, "I will never leave you nor forsake
you" (Heb. 13:5).

The house in Madison Heights was too small for us
now. The three older girls were growing up, and the twins
took their share of space. We told our real estate friend we
were looking for a larger house, and he promised to help.
We listed our house, and the first couple who came to see
it liked it. They spoke German to each other, not knowing I
would understand. I smiled as we walked through the
house, and I listened to their every word. It was no surprise
to me when they said, "We'll take it."

Then I panicked. *Where will we live? We've sold the*

house, but we don't have another to move into. I was conversing with myself, not realizing my heavenly Father understood my need and was supplying it before I even asked.

A few days later, the buyers contacted the real estate agent with the down payment for our house. As the agent called to let me know, he added, "Tania, have Roy call me as soon as he comes home from work. I have a house for you." Roy and I went that same day to see the house—a house that had just been turned over to our friend to sell, and that he had not even had time to list. I loved it. It was an old home in Royal Oak with lots of bedrooms and closets. It was in a nice neighborhood, with an elementary school, middle school, high school, and a park, all within two blocks of the house. To top it off, it was in our price range. Had I known God's Word better at that time, I would have heard Him say, "...before they call, I will answer" (Is. 65:24).

We were happy as we settled into our new home. I had to wait for things I wanted, like new drapes and carpet, but some of those things God supplied in special ways. I had surgery on my feet just after we moved, and Krys told her Sunday school teacher about it. The teacher came to visit, bringing a large box of home-baked cookies. Just to know she cared enough to do that gave me the lift that I needed that day. In our conversation, we discussed my bare living room windows, which had been a trial to me. I had shopped in every store for curtains, but the odd size and shape of the windows made them impossible to fit. The teacher measured them for me that day, and I thought nothing more about it. A few days later, she returned with curtains and rods for those windows. She even hung them for me. I didn't know how to thank her, but she didn't want any thanks. "I love to sew," she said, "and if my talent can bring people joy, that's all the thanks I need." I began to meet more and more people like that, who were a blessing to me, and taught me so much about being a Christian.

Krys had spent eleven years in school in Madison Heights, and she didn't want to transfer in her senior year. We could see no possible solution to the problem, until a neighbor who worked in Madison Heights offered to let Krys ride with him each day to school. Her needs were met, and the desire of her heart granted. I saw God's provision for my children, as well as for Roy and me.

With the larger house, we could now accommodate overnight guests, and we did. Frequently a missionary visited our church, and I volunteered our home for lodging. What a blessing those guests were, and how Roy and I grew in knowledge as those precious Christians shared with us their life experience, while we shared our food and beds with them. It was like a Bible school education, and God knew how needy and hungry my mind was for more of Him.

After the twins' birth, Roy had talked with me about becoming less active in the church, and staying home more. "Honey, I don't believe it is God's will for a wife and mother to be so busy outside the home. I believe He wants you to spend adequate time in rearing the children and teaching them about Him." But I was independent and resistant. Down on my knees I had to go again, reluctantly promising God, for His sake, to obey my husband. I found that it was for my sake too. God poured Himself into me that day, until I felt I could contain no more. He provided an abundance of overnight guests to give me the fellowship and teaching I desired, right in my own home. I obeyed Roy, and curtailed my activities to make my home a priority. I have never been sorry that I did so. The precious memories of the hours and days spent with my children, training them in the ways of the Lord, sustain me even today in times of anxiety about their future.

Eighteen months after the twins were born, Roy went to a friend in the church and asked her, "Ann, will you pray with me for a son?"

"No!" she answered emphatically. "Tania is my friend, and she is busy enough with five children!"

"O.K.," he answered, "I know how to pray for myself now." He began to pray for a son. He told me, "Tania, I don't want to have a son who grows up like me. I want a son to raise to be a great man of God." What do you think happened? You're right—I got pregnant.

Roy took especially good care of me, never letting me lift heavy things, or work too hard. When he went to work he would warn me, "Now don't hurt yourself. Don't let anything happen to the baby." He knew how active and independent I was, and tried to frighten me into being extra careful while he was away.

At the eighth month of pregnancy I went for my regular Friday doctor's appointment. "Everything is just fine, Mrs. Kauppila," he said. On Saturday, I started having pains, and by Sunday I felt really sick. I wondered, *Is this baby coming early?* Monday, while Roy was working, I was rushed into emergency, and had a beautiful baby boy— stillborn.

How I wept! I was afraid to have them call Roy, knowing how disappointed he would be. But when he walked into my room, he smiled and gently took my hand, "It's O.K., honey," he said. "God knows what He is doing. The little guy would probably have grown up to be just like me."

"I would have wanted him to be just like the man you are now, honey!" I sobbed.

We didn't pray for any more children after that. The death of that little boy in 1965 had been a crowning sorrow, and we didn't want to go through that again. Imagine Roy's surprise when I said to him a few months later, "Honey, take me to the doctor. I think I am pregnant!"

Roy looked shocked as we returned home, the pregnancy confirmed.

"How can it be?" he asked. "I was so sure it was not God's will for us to have any more children." I just smiled.

It was romance all over again. Roy was like a young man. He hugged me and kissed me, and again took special care of me. On September 30, 1966, God gave Roy and me a son—a healthy, little blond boy, Matt Roy Kauppila—to delight his parents' hearts. It was the second miracle from a woman's body that supposedly had been surgically rendered incapable of bearing children. "With God, nothing shall be impossible," I whispered.

As our family grew in number we also grew in the Lord. Our church fed us spiritually, cared for us, and provided our Christian education and our entertainment. Both Krys and Lilly met their future husbands in our church, and it was a real blessing to see them both married there. Showers and receptions were all new to me, but Christian friends helped me with it all. I almost forgot my longing for my real mother and father during those years—God so wonderfully provided substitutes.

It was during this time that groups within our church began to ask me to tell my story to them—first in some of the adult Sunday school classes, then for various women's organizations. Soon other churches invited me to do the same for them. Roy and I prayed together about it, and he encouraged me to take this on as a ministry outside the home, as God would lead. It was humbling to think that God was willing to use even me, Tania, with my combined Russian-German-Polish accent! Each time I was allowed to minister in this way, I wanted God to have all the glory, and claim none for myself. Just at the time when the invitations grew numerous, our life changed abruptly.

Roy had gone into partnership with a Christian painter in

Detroit, and finally quit his mill job to do interior decorating full-time. When the partner decided to sell his share of the business and move out-of-state, Roy was able to buy it. Only it didn't turn out the way we expected it to. The business was struggling, since larger painting contractors had been underbidding Roy's former partner. Roy became very discouraged.

It was at this time that our little ones had to be bused to faraway schools, instead of walking to the neighborhood school just two blocks away. This troubled Roy even further. And so, the decision was made in August, 1972 to move to a small community in the northern part of Michigan's Lower Peninsula.

God helped us to find a good-sized piece of land outside Pellston and build a new home on it. We used the money from the sale of our home in Royal Oak. We had high hopes of starting an interior decorating business of our own in the new town, in cooperation with local contractors. They all were optimistic when talking to Roy.

I began to get invitations from churches and Christian women's clubs and women's retreats from all over that part of Michigan, and even from across the big Mackinac Bridge in the Upper Peninsula. Our children adjusted happily to the rural area too, and we got a dog, a few ducks, and some chickens. There were fields to play in and woods to investigate. It seemed as if we had found our place at last.

There were a few regrets, though. We had to leave our church family behind. We found new fellowships to belong to, and to minister within, but we missed our home church tremendously. We also had to leave our three oldest girls behind. Lilly had married shortly after Krys, and Ruthie had been accepted into surgical technician's training, and was happy in her work. I cried as I left them, just as my mother had when I left her, but I knew they had lives of their own to live. I knew we could talk by telephone when the loneliness grew, and we were not too many hours away by car.

For about three years everything went smoothly for us. Then business began to slack off. The rising inflation made people reluctant to remodel. It was a dispensable item—something that could be put off. When Roy could no longer support the family in this way, he made an agonizing decision. He would work in Detroit. Because he had made his mark in his field, a large decorating firm hired him immediately.

All that winter, the family tearfully helped him pack up on Sunday afternoons, and sent him off for a lonely week in the city. I prayed constantly for him, as he was rooming alone in a district where a murder a night was not uncommon. I knew that he drove fearfully, in a locked car with windows rolled up, to and from job assignments. I worried and chafed under the role of mother and father that I had to assume all week. "O God, what have we done?" I prayed. "Have we gotten out of Your will?" We had wanted to do and be all that God would want, but we were not happy. Life was not going well for us. Then it got worse.

I started getting severe chest pains at the least excitement or strain of overwork. The doctor decided it was being caused by a faulty heart valve. As if that were not enough, I developed severe headaches. The local doctors diagnosed the source as tension caused from worry. I believed them, even though the pain got increasingly worse. However, when I began to have trouble seeing, and told Roy, he insisted on an examination by an eye specialist. We went to a doctor in a well-known clinic in a nearby town. He gave us the bad news. "Mrs. Kauppila," he said, "you have a growth on the optic nerve which is inoperable. You also have glaucoma. I can treat only the glaucoma."

Roy immediately wanted to take me to the Mayo Clinic in Minnesota for a second opinion. "Honey," he said, "your eye is important. I think we should see if anything more can be done."

He called long distance to the Mayo Clinic to make an appointment, and the person who answered explained that a referral from a local doctor was necessary, the earliest date I could expect an appointment was three months away, and this length wait was not uncommon. The only other alternative was to just come, and be available in the waiting room in case someone failed to show up, or called to cancel an appointment.

Roy thought this over. "If we just come, how long might the wait be?" He was told it could be three days, or three weeks. Nothing would be certain. Roy said, "Let's go, honey. What do we have to lose?"

A Christian lady came to stay with the children. It took us one full day to make the trip. We got our motel room, and were up early the next morning to drive to the clinic. It was a huge complex. We were directed to the eye clinic, in "seven west." The huge, crowded waiting room reminded me of an airport. People came and went; nurses and receptionists bustled about, telephones rang; voices called patients' names. It was interesting just to sit there, and watch the people, and try to guess what part of the world they were from. We spoke to people from Argentina and from Africa, who were waiting for treatment of serious eye conditions.

Name after name was called out, but not "Kauppila." The morning passed and the afternoon was rapidly coming to an end. Everyone seemed to be showing up for their appointments.

I wasn't just sitting there waiting, feeling sorry for myself, or being depressed. I was praying: "Dear Lord, how thankful I am that You helped us to come over here. I pray that You will give us the right doctor. I pray, Lord, that You will open the way, so we won't have to be sitting here for the next two or three days, or even three weeks. We can't, Lord, and You know why. I don't have to tell You. You know all about it."

It was almost five o'clock that first day when the nurse came into the waiting room and called, "Teena Kapeela." I jumped two feet off the floor, because I couldn't believe my ears. The first day—not even the second or third day, let alone three weeks! And who cared if she mispronounced the name!

The nurse was speaking to me, "Someone just cancelled." She took me into a room, and began administering the test, the first in a series of three that I would need. I was crying so hard that she had difficulty testing me. I was overwhelmed at the knowledge of how the Lord was undertaking for me.

The nurse told me, "I'm glad you could have this test today. Now, you mustn't set your hopes on getting out of the clinic right away. You need two more very important tests. It might mean that you'll have to stay another day or two, maybe even two or three weeks."

I was praying as she administered the test: "Dear Lord, I know You brought me over here. I belong to You, my good right eye, and my bad left eye. You opened the way for this appointment. Perhaps You'll open the way for the other tests even today. You have miracles to give."

Before my first test was over, a young woman walked into the room. "Is this Tania?"

"Yes, it is."

"Did you hear the telephone ring? A lady from out of town can't make her appointment, so when you are through here, send Tania to me." That was my second appointment, and I began crying so hard the nurse had to stop.

"We can't finish the test while you are crying!"

"I'm sorry. But the Lord is being so good to me, that my heart is full of praise."

The second test was a crucial one, because it would point to the exact spot of the growth, and indicate its size. When it was over, I went back to the waiting room to give the news to Roy.

"Honey, I not only had the first test, but also the second one. We still might have to stay two or three days. But imagine! Two tests in one day!"

"If you could have the other one tomorrow, Tania, we could go back home. I have just enough money for one more night in a motel and gasoline to get home."

I was describing the tests to Roy when the doctor came into the waiting room and said to the nurse, "The next patient is a little bit late. Just go ahead and start working on Tania."

Roy looked at me and gave me a little hug, and I went across the hall for my last test. By that time I was so overcome at God's goodness to me that I walked into the room, put my head on my lap, and cried and praised the Lord. The patient whose place I was taking never did show up or call to cancel.

When the test was completed, I went back to wait with Roy. Then we were both called into a conference room, where several doctors were seated around a table. They took their time to explain carefully about the optic nerve. The growth on mine was very serious; they were not able to tell how long the growth had been there, but explained that it was a type that would grow very slowly. They concurred with the diagnosis of the local specialist that it was inoperable. There was the possibility that it could eventually lead to blindness.

By this time it was almost 8:00 P.M., and the Lord had arranged all of those three tests to be done in three hours. What a miracle!

As we drove back to Pellston the following day, our hearts were full of praise. There were misgivings about my eye condition. But how precious was the knowledge that our God of miracles was in complete control!

24

Upheaval

Trust in the Lord with all your heart,
And lean not on your own understanding;
In all your ways acknowledge Him,
And he shall direct your paths (Prov. 3:5–6).

When we first moved to Pellston in 1972, Tania and Nina were fourth-graders, and Matt was beginning the first grade.

We loved the tiny church we attended. Many times during the winter, our congregation consisted of only three families. The fellowship was especially close and sweet. During the summer, when families migrated north to their summer cottages, our congregation swelled to sixty or seventy people. We always looked forward to their coming. Everyone knew everyone else. Being active in our little church was an important part of our lives, and we knew the Lord was using us there.

Even as the economy became worse in northern Michigan, the children were content. They had friends and activities that kept them busy. They literally lived in the outdoors, exploring the woods near our home. Tania and Nina knew the names of all the trees and wild flowers. They and their friends knew the edible mushrooms, and just where to look for them. Matt's constant companion was his dog, Dusty, who was always trailing along, ready for a romp in the woods.

During this time, of course, Roy had been commuting

back and forth to Detroit. One day Lilly, who was married and had a daughter by then, called him: "Dad, why don't you give up that room and come out to Garden City to stay with Jeff and me during the week? It'll give Jennifer a chance to get better acquainted with her grandpa too." Roy lost no time in making the arrangements—we both felt better about having him there. I knew he was lonely, and it would be good for him to be with part of our family. Four-year-old Jennifer would know how to keep Grandpa occupied!

The economy was beginning to worsen in southern Michigan by this time, and the company Roy worked for was getting fewer contracts. Since Roy was the last one hired, his hours were the first to be cut. One week, when things were especially slow, he walked into the house with this morose greeting: "Well, I spent the last of the money I made this week on gasoline to get home. We can't go on like this. I'm going to have to look for another job and cut out all this driving. I'm going to look for a house to rent down there—this trying to live in two places is beginning to get to me. I know you love this place, honey, and I do, too. But enough is enough!"

Tears came unbidden to my eyes as I thought, *O Lord, did You give us this beautiful little home just to take it away from us again? Our family is being used in our little church. You have given me a speaking ministry up here. What is there for us in the Detroit area?*

During the week, as I was driving down to Midland, Michigan, for a speaking engagement, I was still praying that the Lord would intervene in our behalf. God, in His faithfulness, was preparing to do just that, but not in the way that I had been asking.

Midland was just about the halfway point between Detroit and the tip of northern Michigan. Three precious friends had arranged to drive up from Detroit to be present at the meeting. Afterward, we attempted to catch up on all of our news. Finally Anne asked, "Tania, how are things really going for you and Roy up north?"

I shook my head. "Not good at all. Roy has been commuting back and forth between Detroit and Pellston for some time now. We haven't discussed it with the children as yet, but we may have to sell the house and move back to Detroit. Roy's actually looking for a house to rent this week. He's that serious about it."

"Oh!" broke in Mary. "There is a young couple from our church going on a year's term as missionaries to Peru. They want to rent their completely furnished home while they are gone. They are taking only their clothing and a few household articles with them. Tell us how to reach Roy, and we'll let him know about it. If he is interested, the place is available."

We finally said our goodbyes, and I turned to go back to Pellston. Could this be the Lord's answer to our prayer? As He said, "...before they call, I will answer;/And while they are still speaking, I will hear" (Is. 65:24).

When I finally pulled into the driveway, I sat for a moment, enjoying the view of our nearby woods. I never tired of watching the beauty of each season—the haze of green in the boughs as the first hint of spring appeared; the leaves unfurling like tiny flags to produce the mysterious cloak of summer; the gold and crimson of the autumn leaves mixing and then falling to the ground; even the stark beauty of the trees in winter gave a Christmas-card effect with the snow swirling around. How could anyone want to live elsewhere? Could we really leave this little home we had built? Leave the open spaces we had all learned to love? Leave my little Sunday school class to another teacher? I resolved not to think about it anymore. If Roy rented a house, it would be soon enough to tell the children. Let them enjoy themselves as long as possible.

Early in the week Roy called: "It's done. I have been able to make arrangements to lease the missionaries' house. Go ahead and tell the children our plans, and then start packing. You can be ready when I come this weekend, can't you, Tania?"

"Oh, Roy! So *soon*? How will I ever be able to break the news to the children! Yes, honey, we will try our very best to be ready when you come."

School was due to begin the following week. Tania and Nina would be freshmen in high school. Matt would be in the sixth grade. How would they take the news? Matt didn't seem concerned, but the girls were another matter. I could see the storm of consternation gathering on their faces. "Moving!" they cried in unison. "Moving! What do you mean, we are moving! School starts next week. We *can't* move!" And they ran howling to their room to bewail their plight together in privacy.

Meanwhile, Matt had slipped out the back door, and I looked out to see where he was. With his back to me, I couldn't tell how he really felt about it, but there he sat, hunched up, chin resting on his knees, looking out toward the woods. Dusty knew his master had come outside, and came racing to where Matt was sitting, as if to say, "Come on, Matt! Let's go look for squirrels! We might even see a fox or two. But we sure know enough to stay away from the porcupines and skunks, don't we? C'mon! Let's go for a romp!"

Sensing Matt's mood, Dusty lowered his head, and with tail wagging slowly, came to join Matt, and reached over to lick his face. A moment later, Matt lunged for Dusty, and then boy and dog were one ball of activity, rolling over and over on the grass. *Thank You, Lord,* I thought. *Matt will manage.*

It was a busy week, and as we worked, I attempted to explain that Roy was trying to do the very best for his family that he knew how to do. "Please, girls, don't let your father see you are upset. He doesn't want to make this move any more than we do. Let's just thank the Lord for a father who wants to support you, and to care for you."

Things seemed to be going well, and we began preparing our clothes for packing. Then I walked by their closed bedroom door and heard sobbing. "Tania! Nina! What is the matter?" Silence. "Girls! Can't you tell Mother what is the matter?"

"*You* know what the matter is! You're taking us away from all our friends. They will all be together and we'll never see them again! It's O.K. for you and Dad. You know *millions* of people down there, but we don't know anyone at all! We will have to start high school in a new school where we don't know *anyone*!

"But, girls, you have each other. You won't be alone. And you will be able to make lots of friends, in addition to the friends you have here. You'll see." And with that, the sobs began again.

The weekend arrived, and Roy was home. I sent up a quick prayer that the Lord would help us not to be teary-eyed before Roy. I knew it would be difficult, knowing we were spending the last weekend in our home. Saying goodbye to our church family would not be much easier.

Roy walked in and looked around. "Hi! How are things going? Everyone about packed?"

"Hi, Dad. Just about." I was so pleased to see the girls' efforts not to appear unhappy this last weekend. Matt seemed his usual self. As we ate supper, Roy had much to tell us. He had a new job, working in the maintenance department of a large hospital. He explained that the house in which we would live was located in the same school district where Krystina, Lilly, and Ruthie had attended high school. Tania, Nina, and Matt would be able to graduate from that same high school. We would be just a few minutes from our home church. There would be a lot of special activities there for the children to take part in. We would be able to see Krystina, Lilly, Ruthie, and their families on a regular basis. If Roy noticed that everyone seemed quieter than usual, he did not comment on it.

The next day at church, I treasured each smile, each handclasp from our dear friends. I soaked up every word from our dear pastor, and remembered his faithfulness to God's Word, whether there were fifteen people present, or seventy. I thought of the many times of fellowship we had shared and of the many picnics we had had with them and with all our church family on our home property. With fifty acres, there was plenty of room for softball or football. Our goodbyes were tearful.

At last we were on our way home, and as we pulled into the driveway, we heard Roy say, "Everyone get a good night's sleep tonight, because we will be packing the station wagon and pickup the first thing in the morning. Hopefully we will beat some of the heavy southbound Labor Day traffic."

"Get a good night's sleep." Was that what Roy had said? So many thoughts were bouncing around in my head. I thought of each person to whom we had said goodbye today. Then I thought of the happy times we had spent in this house. It seemed an interminable time before my mind would cooperate with my body, and allow it to relax and sleep.

Morning came all too quickly, and we were caught up in the activity of actually packing the vehicles for our moving day.

"Now, Tania, Matt and I will be riding in the pickup. Let me take the lead when we get out on the highway. Try to keep close enough behind me to discourage anyone's pulling in between us. I don't want us to lose each other in the traffic. And, honey, when we pull away from the house, please don't look back. Just keep coming."

We gathered together and asked the Lord to grant safety for us on the highway, and to protect our unoccupied house from vandalism. Then Roy and Matt climbed into the truck and prepared to pull away from the house. The girls and I climbed into the car, and I backed out of the driveway. Here was one little house, isolated on its own fifty acres, a few miles out from town, and we were leaving it, completely furnished. It needed God's protection!

"Don't look back. Just keep coming." With Roy's words still in my mind, I found myself turning for just "one last look." "Oh! Such a beautiful little home!" My head dropped to the steering wheel, as the tears came. I could hear the girls crying quietly in the back seat. Then, knowing that Roy was waiting for me to get started, we pulled out behind them, and onto the highway. I wept as I drove, thinking of this upheaval as one more thing that had happened in my hard life. *O Lord, why this on top of everything else?*

The Lord allowed me to commiserate with myself for a period of time, then began gently placing his thoughts in my mind.

"Tania, My dear child, have you placed too much importance on that house? Do you love that house more than you love Me?"

"Oh, no, Lord, You are first in my thoughts!"

"Can you remember the months you traveled with your family as refugees, with no home at all, and only the clothes that were on your back? Do you remember the thousands who died of starvation? Did I care for you then?"

"Oh, yes, Lord; I know how it was only Your care that brought us through that time."

"Now, Tania, you are traveling with most of your family to another home that I have provided for you. You will be closer to the rest of your family, whom you love. Do you remember another trip taken in a boxcar, to an unknown destination, completely away from all your family and friends? Did I not care for you then? Can I not care for you now? Can you not forget these 'things' and just follow after Me in faith?"

"Yes, Lord. Forgive me, Father. Help me to be an encouragement to my husband and my children in this move. Help me to keep my eyes only on You."

It was so quiet in the back seat that I glanced in the mirror, and saw the reason. Both girls were sleeping. They looked so peaceful, even angelic, lying there.

My mind flew back to when they were babies. I thought of times when I had pushed them in their twin-stroller and heard someone exclaim, "Oh, oh. Double trouble!" My answer was always, "No, no; double blessing." I remembered how curly their brown hair was from birth. And I remembered their blue, blue eyes—blue until they were five years old, that is, when within one week our blue-eyed twins became brown-eyed ones! What a surprise that was to everyone.

"Girls, wake up; I see your father is signaling to pull off the expressway. Matt must have talked him into stopping for something to eat."

"Good. Dad must know we're really empty."

Everyone's spirits seemed buoyed up, and I could sense an excitement in the children. This move was not of their choosing, but now that we were nearing our destination, they were beginning to feel a sense of adventure. Stopping to stretch cramped muscles, and feed hungry tummies was part of it, I am sure.

Soon we were back on the road, and as the miles sped

by, Tania and Nina were no longer sleepy, but were filled with questions and observations.

"Do you think anyone will like us? What will we do if no one likes us?"

Without an answer, or even discussion, would come another question:

"I wonder what it will be like to live in a city, with a house right next door on each side? I liked it being far away from other houses."

"I wonder how far away from school we will be?"

"Do you suppose we'll ever have another house of our own?"

And then, there it was, the little house in which we would be spending almost a year. The lawn was freshly mowed, and everything looked so neat. What if Dusty were to tear up that beautiful lawn? We would have to train that dog to walk carefully here. This was not the wide-open space of Pellston!

As we carried suitcases into the house, we began peering about the rooms, wanting the strangeness of this new place to fade away. The first job to be done was to get all of the beds made up for five exhausted Kauppilas. Then I discovered the reason for Roy's big grin. He had made up all the beds before he came to Pellston to pick us up!

"Surprise, honey. I knew how tired we'd all be when we got here."

I gave him a grateful hug. How good it felt to be able just to climb into bed. As I looked around the unfamiliar room, I thought, *So much has happened today. We have been transplanted into a new house, with new experiences awaiting us.* Tonight, I purposed in my mind to stay awake and plan the myriad of things that needed to be done tomorrow, but in spite of my resolve, my brain was growing increasingly fuzzy.

Then the thoughts that I had refused to think about forced their way into my mind. *How would we be able to continue paying the mortgage on the home in Pellston until it was sold? What if it did not sell right away? Could Roy's salary stretch that far? Would we end up losing the place for non payment?* Roy and I would have to make a decision quickly on what to do.

25

A New Ministry

✳

For I am not ashamed of the gospel of Christ, for it is the power of God to salvation for everyone who believes, for the Jew first and also for the Greek (Rom. 1:16).

It was Labor Day of 1977 when we moved to Royal Oak, a northern suburb of Detroit. The following Sunday, Roy and I happily began renewing friendships at our church. At the same time, we were busily encouraging the girls and Matt to make friends, and to make the plunge into the church's youth activities.

The next few days were a flurry of activity. The most important thing of course, was to register the children in their new schools. I could see their curious looks at this new environment. The twins were spending a lot of time in their bedroom, and coming out with the tell-tale signs of weeping. Matt seemed to take the change stoically.

How we thanked God for the Youth Minister and his wife, Gordy and Phyllis. Their faithfulness in spending hours with the teens in conducting Bible studies, in counseling with them, and in sharing recreational times, made a real spiritual impact on our children. Roy and I could see Tania, Nina, and Matt being absorbed into their peer groups.

Only after the initial things were done to establish us in our new home could I begin to think about our future and our finances. I needed to broach this special subject with

Roy, and I did not know how he would react. That day when we knelt together in the kitchen, and I promised to quit my job and allow Roy to care for me and our family, I had meant it. Roy had cared for us, and I knew it. But now there was a rental check to be made each month, in addition to a mortgage payment on our Pellston home. Until the home was sold, I wanted to help Roy. Would he allow me to? Or would he feel it a slur against his ability to care for us?

After praying about it, I approached Roy, and asked how he would feel if I were to go back to work until our home up north would be sold. Roy was quiet for a minute. "You know, honey, I've been thinking about our financial situation, and trying to decide if I can get another job, and work two jobs. As tired as I am when I come home, I don't think that I could do it, at least, not for very long. I know I promised you that you would never have to work outside the home again, but I do need help right now. I don't know how I can do it alone. If you really feel you want to get a job, it would help us. What kind of job were you thinking about?"

I hadn't even considered what kind of job, or where, but Ruthie had worked at the hospital several years, and so I decided to ask her if there might be a hospital job I could do.

"What about working in the dietary kitchen, Mom? You always were interested in food!"

I laughed. Ruthie certainly knew her mother. Roy brought home an application, and together we filled it out, and then he took it back to the hospital with him. During the time of waiting to hear from the hospital, I had second thoughts. *Should I be doing this? Is there another way to help Roy? Maybe another kind of job would be better for me to do. Will I even be accepted?*

By the time I received a call to come in for an interview, I was really shaking. When I heard, "The job is yours, Mrs.

Kauppila," I could hardly wait to share the news with my family.

There was so much to learn at the beginning, that I hardly had time to notice the people I was working with. But I did notice that they were all young enough to be my children.

The assigned lunch breaks were 11:00–11:30, and 11:30–12:00. As we all sat together at lunch, or on our break time, I began to get acquainted with them as individuals.

One of the first I got to know was Nita. She was a lovely young girl, with blonde hair.

"Do you go to college, Nita?"

"No, I worked in a convalescent home, and put my application in here, and got the job. I like it a lot better."

"Are you married, engaged, or what?"

"Well, I'm not married, or engaged, so I guess it's 'what.' I live with my boyfriend, to see if it works out or not. We've lived together a couple of years or so."

I was quiet, and praying silently, "Dear Lord, what do I do now? Please give me the wisdom I need."

"Nita, I think you are a beautiful girl. Would you let me give you my opinion?"

Nita shrugged her shoulders. "Sure, why not?"

"If you were my daughter, I would tell you *no*. Marriage is honorable in God's sight, regardless of where you get married. But you are not married, and that is what the Bible terms 'living in sin.' "

She shrugged her shoulders again. "I know. So what?"

That was it. I quit talking about it. But I asked the Lord to help me be a testimony to her, and to give her love and kindness.

After that, she did her best to pick on me, making snide remarks to me when she could. She hadn't liked what I had said! I kept praying that the Lord would give me more love for her; that Nita would drown in the love the Lord would give me for her. Gradually, when she saw that I said nothing more to her about her living arrangement, she began to soften toward me.

One day I asked, "Nita, how would you like to go with me for a few days up north? I go periodically to check on our home in Pellston. The next time we both have the same days off, would you like to go? You can be my guest."

"Sure, why not?"

Two or three weeks later, we ended up having the same days off, and began our trip up north. I had my Bible lying on the seat between us as we drove. While we were in conversation, if I happened to think of a Bible verse that was on the subject we were discussing, I would give her the reference and say, "Look it up, Nita, and read it to me." As I was driving I would direct her where to find it, and she would read it to me aloud. All the time I was praying that the Holy Spirit would use the Word to grip her mind and heart.

We spent the weekend together, and it was my joy to lead her to the Lord. She told me of a time years before when she was attending a school Bible club, and had prayed "some kind of prayer." She came from a broken home, and her life as a youngster had been an unhappy one.

Nita continued living with her boyfriend. She told me they were even buying furniture together. I was praying the Lord would break up that situation somehow, to allow Nita to grow in the Lord, and that Nita would have the wisdom to tell her boyfriend that they must separate.

They were eventually separated, but in a tragic way. One day she told me that he was in another hospital, suffering from a staph infection. Within three weeks he died. Some of us from the hospital visited the funeral home, and there sat Nita by his coffin, weeping. It was my first glimpse of him, a very handsome young man, about twenty-two years of age. Later Nita told me he had been a "real tough cookie"—that his staph infection was from shooting heroin. He had been a pusher, had stolen money for his drug habit, and had been in and out of jail.

I saw Nita not more than a year ago, at one of our church concerts. She was bubbling over with love for the Lord. She was still single. She was attending a Bible study, basking in the new knowledge the Lord was bringing to her. How thankful I am every time I think of Nita!

When the "kitchen gang" would sit together for lunch or our break, one thing really bothered me. It seemed all these young people were hooked on cigarettes. The kitchen was so hot, that when I sat at a table, I wanted to breathe fresh air instead of smoke.

"Guys, don't puff on me! The Lord gave us lungs, and He wants us to breathe fresh air! If you're going to do that, I'm going to sit by myself."

"Oh, no, no, don't do that, Tania. Stay here with us. We want you here with us."

One of the boys was Mike, a handsome boy, not too long out of high school. He had a job scrubbing pots and pans eight hours a day. I couldn't see much future in this! As I would take dirty pans to him, and get clean ones, I would say, "Hi, Mike, how're things going?"

He would always swear about the "same old pots and pans."

"Come on, Mike, don't complain. You have a job, and two hands to do it. Maybe later you can ask God to give you another job. In the meantime, you have a paycheck coming in."

I could see Mike was becoming attached to me. "Hey, Tania, what time is your lunch today?"

"Eleven-thirty."

"Is it O.K. if I have lunch with you?"

"Sure; I'll even buy you lunch."

During one lunch with Mike, he said, "I have a question for you, Tania. I have a girlfriend; we've been going together for a couple years now, and we're living together in my apartment. What do you think about that?"

"No, Mike!"

"What do you mean?"

"You heard me. Don't do it! I'm surprised at you!" I could talk to Mike rougher than I did to Nita, because boys seem to like to have it told like it is, with no beating around the bush. I said to him, "Mike, if you were my son, I would tell you *no*. That is not the way God wants it."

"Well, she's a beautiful girl, but I don't know if I want to get stuck with her."

"You're not going to find out by living with her. Do you want to marry her?"

"I don't know."

"You *know*, you know! If you wanted to marry her, you would have married her before now. You just want to use her. No boy wants to live with a girlfriend and then marry her. Do you think another boy will want to marry her after you have lived with her? No! He will think she is only good enough to live with someone else, not to marry. You've ruined her life and yours. Get away from her. Break up. That's wrong. You're hearing it from me right now, that it's wrong."

"My father doesn't care."

"Well, God does!"

He shrugged his shoulders. "Well..."

I tried to witness to him and tell him that God gave him life to begin with, and had a great purpose for that life. God loved him so much that He sent Jesus to die for him, and for all his sins—one of which he was living right now.

Mike did break up with the girl, and she moved out of

his apartment. I invited him to church, and he began coming. Imagine my joy when I saw him walk forward to give his life to the Lord.

All the young people began talking to me on my lunch hour. I would grab a cup of coffee or a glass of water, and sit there as they came to ask questions of me, and ask counsel. I thank the Lord that He opened up this avenue of ministry for me.

One of my kitchen duties was to prepare and sterilize the baby food served to hospitalized infants. A heavy cast-iron wheel must be turned to either open or close the sterilizer. Usually two or three women worked together to manipulate this wheel, when none of our strong young men were there to do it for us. One particular day, no one was nearby, so I just decided to do it alone. *Surely I can turn this wheel by myself,* I thought. As it began to turn, my hand slipped, my shoulder hit the wall, and I suffered a bruise. Nothing to worry about. As required, I reported the incident, and had my shoulder X-rayed, showing no damage. My arm was black-and-blue, but I knew it would feel better once the bruise faded. I favored my right arm while the bruise healed, but the pain persisted. The doctor had me begin ultrasound therapy. *Is my shoulder becoming arthritic?* I wondered.

Working in the Dietary Kitchen was becoming an ordeal. I decided to ask for a transfer to some other department where the physical labor would be less taxing for my shoulder. A few weeks later, an opening did come up in another department, and it came time to say goodbye to the "Kitchen gang." I would miss each one of them. The Lord had allowed a ministry for me there. Would there be a ministry in the new department?

The word had gone ahead of me to the new department that I was a "very religious lady." One of the first things I heard was, "Oh! You are religious. We have Louise, and she's religious, too. The two of you should get along well together!" And we did. It was a joy knowing her.

Anna, another lady, came to me with questions concerning what she was hearing taught at her church. I would always tell her what the Bible said, not what I thought about it. We had rich fellowship when we were able to have lunch together. I was always very careful to have any discussions about spiritual things on my lunch hour, or my break, never during my working hours.

Then there was Nickie. She carefully avoided being around me whenever possible. I began praying for her. I wanted to win her to the Lord.

When we found ourselves together at lunch, almost the first thing she said to me was, "I know you don't believe in what I'm doing. I'm living with Tom, but so what? Just don't preach to me, and we'll get along just fine."

"Well, that's your life, Nickie. Nobody's going to make you change your way of living. But since you realize what you are doing is wrong, you're not going to be happy, regardless of what you say. You're a beautiful girl. You don't need to live with him!"

"I couldn't stand living with my father and my mother at home. They nag me."

"It would be better to stay at home even if they do nag you. If they nag, do they have a reason for it?"

She soon became very precious to me. No longer did she try to avoid me. My words to her were: "It's up to you, but I still want to tell you what God says is right or wrong."

I didn't win Nickie to the Lord. But I did tell her what to do with her life, and left it like that. My prayer is that God will one day use those words to draw her to Himself.

26

A Time of Uncertainty

*

And my God shall supply all your need according to His riches in glory by Christ Jesus (Phil. 4:19).

During the first year that I was working at the hospital, Roy and I began looking in the newspaper to see what homes were for sale. We knew the time would come when we would have to vacate the Barringtons' home, and we hoped that at that time we would be able to move into a home of our own. We certainly hoped that the Pellston home would be sold soon, to enable us to have a down payment on a new home, were we to find one quickly. Everything we saw listed in the newspaper seemed to be out of our price range, besides being too far away from where we wanted to locate. We carried pictures of our Pellston home with us to show to all our friends, hoping we would get a lead on someone in the market for a beautiful home up north.

One day at church a dear friend greeted me—one I didn't get to talk to too often. She asked how things were going with our family.

"Pretty good, Reneé. The children were crushed when we told them we would be moving away from Pellston, but they have been making friends, and seem to be very happy here. You know that we are staying in the Barringtons' home this year while they are in Peru serving as missionaries.

They are due to be home soon, and we will have to move again. We had hoped to be able to buy a home, rather than to rent or lease another one. We keep looking in the newspapers, but so far have not found anything."

"Oh, Tania! You know, don't you, that my husband, Ted, is now a real estate agent. He obtained his license while you were living up north. He works for the Graham agency. Would you like to have me ask him to help you look for a home?"

We were happy to talk to Ted, to describe for him what we felt we could afford, and the location in which we were interested. We were trusting that the Lord would allow the Pellston home to be sold soon, in order to provide a down payment on another house when we found one.

The day drew nearer when we would have to vacate the Barringtons' home, and we realized we were no nearer to finding a home, or selling the one up north. We began looking for a place, hoping to be able to rent it by the month, rather than to have to sign a lease for it. It seemed everyone wanted a year's lease when they rented their homes. Finally, we found a tiny place in Birmingham, northwest of Royal Oak, and began trying to persuade the landlord to allow us to sign just a three-month lease. We explained that we were in the process of looking for a home to buy, and did not want to be tied down by a year's lease. He would not consider anything shorter than a six-month lease, so we finally agreed to his terms, feeling we had no other choice.

This was an unfurnished home, and so besides bringing our personal belongings from where we were living, we also had to move some furniture from our Pellston home. We left early one morning. When we reached Pellston, Roy hired some boys from the area to help him pack furniture into the truck. By the time we reached Birmingham, late that night in June, 1978, we were all exhausted. Angels of mercy, in the form of the members of our Sunday school class, came the next afternoon, and helped Roy unload the truck. We thanked God for our very special friends. The home in Pellston had not been sold. Somehow, we had felt that the Lord would work another miracle by having it sold, to provide us with the down payment to make on another house, before having to sign another lease.

By this time, Roy was experiencing some health problems, and was under a doctor's care. Several types of medication had been prescribed for him, even one for his nerves. I could begin to see the telltale signs of discouragement and depression in Roy. Often when I greeted him as he came in from work, with "Hi, Roy; how was your day?" his answer would be just a grunt, or "Don't ask," or "Who cares?"

Tania's old nature would flare up, and I would think to myself, *Big deal! I am a wage earner, too, in this house. I come home tired, too.* And I would begin to enumerate mentally what *I* had to do, then begin silently to commiserate with myself.

Ted called one day to tell us about a house. "It is an older home, in the price range you are looking for, and in the school district where your older girls attended high school. Why don't you meet me there?"

Roy and I agreed, and left to meet him at the house. We arrived before Ted. As we parked in front of the house, we looked at the neighborhood, and decided it looked friendly and neat. We liked what we could see of the house, from the outside. A couple was sitting in the enclosed sunporch, and Roy decided to let them know that we were waiting to meet the real estate agent there.

"Come in; come on in! We can talk while you are waiting." He introduced his wife and himself as the Marlowes. Now that he was retired from the police force, he and his wife wanted to sell their home to buy another in Kalamazoo,

Michigan, to be near their daughter and her family. We chatted for a few minutes, and then Mr. Marlowe looked at me quizzically.

"I detect an accent in your speech. May I ask where you are from?"

I could see the surprise in his face as I answered, "I was born the first time in Kiev, Russia, and the second time in Ford Hospital, Detroit, Michigan."

"Wait a minute. What are you talking about, 'born a second time'? That's not possible."

I told him a tiny part of my life story, and explained that when I came to the realization that I, like everyone else, was a sinner, I asked God to forgive my sin through the blood of Jesus Christ, shed on the cross for me. I then became a Christian, "born again" into God's family.

Mr. Marlowe remarked, "That is quite a story, Mrs. Kauppila."

By this time Ted had arrived, and we began the tour of the house. We knew immediately that we loved it. The house was not overly large, but it would fit our family extremely well. Besides being in the same school district as we had been before moving up north, we would also be just a few minutes from our church. It was important to us to be close to our church, since our children were now very active in the youth program.

We followed Ted back to his office to discuss terms of the sale. The Marlowes wanted seven thousand dollars down on a land contract. Roy said, "You know, Ted, we are still waiting for our home in Pellston to be sold. We never dreamed that it would take this long to sell. You also know that we had to sign a six-month lease where we are living. We had to pay the first and last month in advance, plus the equivalent of one month's rent as a security deposit. All this, besides paying a mortgage payment on the house up north. Seven thousand might as well be seven million. Right now, I don't see how we can touch it."

"Roy, we have an almighty God. He knows about your lease, and He knows about your mortgage payment in Pellston. I personally feel that this is the house for your family's needs. Reneé and I are going to pray that the Lord will enable you to have this house."

As we were driving home, Roy wondered aloud, "Why hasn't our home sold yet? The property is beautiful, and so is the house. I thought it would be snapped right up. Here it has been on the market for over a year. Even with both of us working, I don't see how we can buy this other house. You know we can't break the lease on the house we are in. If we walk out of our agreement, we will lose a good bit of money. That, plus a double mortgage payment, is out of the question. I'm only human. I can't produce money that just is not there. And there is nowhere to go for the money."

By the time we reached home, Roy had decided to call Ted back. "Ted, you'll have to tell the Marlowes that we just can't buy the house. Until our house up north sells, we cannot make a down payment."

"Roy, I've already talked to Mr. Marlowe, and asked if he would accept a lower down payment. He said he could not, but listen to what he did say: 'We want the Russian lady and her husband to have this house. We can tell they really want it. We are willing to wait for them even a year, if necessary, to give them time to raise the down payment. We live close enough to Kalamazoo that we can travel back and forth to see our daughter.' What do you think of that, Roy? You and Tania start praying, and let's see what God will do."

Roy was becoming more withdrawn. More and more, when he came in from work, he would just walk into the bedroom and lie down to rest. And more and more, Tania's old nature would flare up, but only inside. I prided myself that none of my family could tell how angry with Roy I was inside. I would think, *Why do I have to work all day in that hot hospital and then come home to do everything by myself?* I was getting pretty adept at hiding my feelings.

Then one evening Tania came into the kitchen where I was cooking supper and said, "Mom, I think Dad's really sick. You'd better come in and take a look at him."

Yeah, yeah, I thought to myself. *I'll bet he's sick! I'm the one who is sick...sick of him!*

"Mom, Dad's breathing funny, and his face looks funny. You really should come in and look at him."

I turned off the burner under the skillet I was tending, and walked into the bedroom. When I saw Roy, I panicked. "Dear Lord, what is the matter with him!" Roy was gasping for breath. His eyes were rolling about, with a wild, frantic look to them.

I grabbed the yellow pages of the telephone directory. "Ambulance...ambulance...where's the number for one?" My fingers shook as I dialed the number. "Busy! The line to the ambulance company is busy! What shall I do? What shall I do?"

"Mom, just call the operator and ask her to connect you with the Fire Department. They'll get an ambulance here."

Thank the Lord for a daughter who could think clearly in an emergency! The Fire Department assured me they would be there quickly. I was still shaking when the ambulance arrived. The paramedics took over with quiet efficiency, administering oxygen, placing Roy on the gurney, and preparing to take him to the hospital. Thank God, Roy was breathing normally now. And he was conscious, protesting the need to go to the hospital. We overruled him, however, and I followed the medics out to the ambulance.

"Are you sure you are O.K., Mrs. Kauppila? You can ride

in the ambulance, you know, and then have someone pick you up later."

Watching their quick, efficient movements had given me assurance, and by this time I was no longer shaking. I elected to follow them. I wanted to be alone to pray for my husband as I drove. How could I be so angry at my husband one moment, and in sheer panic the next moment, when I feared that he was dying? Was the Lord trying to tell me something? *Speak clearly, please, Lord; make sure I understand.*

Later, at the hospital, when I was finally allowed to see Roy and the doctor, Roy was shaking his head. "I don't know what happened. I felt so jittery and tired when I came home that I took some medication before lying down. Maybe I thought I hadn't taken it, and took it again. I don't know. I'm sorry I caused a problem."

The doctor told me, "Mrs. Kauppila, it's fortunate your daughter noticed what was happening to your husband. In another hour we would not have been able to save him. It was an overdose of medication, but he's fine now, and you may take him home."

Roy and I were both quiet on the way home. I was feeling so ashamed of the mean thoughts I'd had earlier that evening. What if Roy had died before help arrived? But I still argued with myself: *Roy doesn't know what my thoughts were, so I don't need to say anything to him.*

When we reached home, Roy just said, "I think I'll go right to bed if you don't mind, honey."

That was all right with me. My thoughts were in a turmoil; why should I stir up trouble by telling Roy what I had been thinking? When I was sure he was really asleep, I slipped into bed beside him and closed my eyes.

27

Peace After the Storm

✻

...and the peace of God, which surpasses all understanding, will guard your hearts and minds through Christ Jesus (Phil. 4:7).

Roy and I both slept late the next morning. The children had gone on to school by the time we woke up, and I went into the kitchen to fix breakfast for the two of us. Roy, of course, would not be expected at work today. I had left a message at the hospital the night before that I would remain home with Roy.

As we sat at the breakfast table, Roy picked at his food. He had been quiet all morning. Finally, he pushed his plate back, and said, "Honey, I want to ask your forgiveness. I've been so discouraged and frustrated over not being able to make arrangements about a house. It seems that we're just not getting ahead at all. I haven't been treating you and the family right. You have been so patient and understanding, never saying a word. Will you forgive me?"

And then my spirit broke. "Oh, Roy; I need *your* forgiveness! I haven't been patient and understanding at all! I was quiet on the outside, and priding myself that I was keeping my true feelings from you. I have been rebellious and resentful on the inside. Please forgive me!"

And then we were in each other's arms, allowing our tears of repentance to flow together.

"Roy, I need to ask God's forgiveness, too." And I began

pouring out my heart in a prayer that God would forgive me for my pride, and give me a new understanding of my husband's needs, and help me to be the kind of wife I should be. When I finished praying, Roy began to pray, asking God to forgive Him and to help him to be the spiritual leader that we needed in our home. He prayed that we would be given a fresh love for God and for each other, and that God would cleanse our hearts of all bitterness.

Then we were in each other's arms again, thanking God for sparing Roy's life, and for reviving our spirits toward Himself, and toward each other.

"Honey," Roy was saying, "I really do not know what happened with my medication. I wouldn't want to go through an experience like that again. But God has used it to draw us closer to Him and to each other; and for that, I am thankful."

We were still praising the Lord when the telephone rang. I picked it up, and said, "Hello."

A man asked, "Is Roy there, please?" I didn't recognize the voice of the caller. As I called to Roy, I wondered if it might be someone from the hospital to ask how he was feeling today.

When Roy took the call, I saw a big smile cover his face. "Oh, hello! I wasn't expecting to hear from you today." Then the smile left his face, and he sat down suddenly, his eyes growing wide with wonder. "Oh, no, no; I can't let you do that! I just don't know what to say!"

"Do what, Roy? Who is it?" But he just gave me an impatient wave of his hand. He continued listening, shaking his head all the while. Finally he said, "All right; I'm on my way. But I don't know how I am *ever* going to thank you." As he hung up, his whole body seemed to go limp.

"Who was that on the telephone, Roy? What did he want?"

Roy took my hand, and drew me down beside him. Again, he had tears flooding his eyes.

"Honey, remember that verse: 'Before they call, I will answer; and while they are still speaking, I will hear'? Well, that was our friend Jack Larimore calling."

Jack! Why hadn't I recognized his voice? Jack, and Maria his wife, were our friends from near Pellston. Then I hurried to catch up with what Roy was saying:

"...and for a week now, while they have been reading the Bible and praying, the Lord has been bringing us to their minds, and strongly impressing on them that we have a financial need, and that they were to give us a gift of money. Are you ready for this, Tania? Seven thousand dollars!"

I just stared at Roy, hardly comprehending what he was saying. Jack and Maria wanted to give us a gift of seven thousand dollars? Had Roy really said that? There was no way they could have known the exact amount that we needed. We had not shared with anyone that we were praying for the down payment for a house. Then we were laughing and crying and hugging each other, as we basked in the knowledge of this new miracle the Lord was giving to us.

"Roy! Call Ted and tell him what has happened." Roy's fingers were trembling with emotion as he dialed Ted's number and waited for him to answer.

"Ted, this is Roy. I have to tell you about the miracle that has just happened. God is giving us the seven thousand dollars for the down payment on the house! Can you believe that? Friends of ours from near Pellston have just called, and offered it to us. I am leaving within the hour to pick it up."

Then Roy pulled the receiver away from his ear as the voice of Ted excitedly rang out. "Well, praise the *Lord!* Reneé and I have been praying daily that the Lord would enable you to buy that house. Hal-le-*lu*-jah! He is a prayer-answering God, isn't He?"

I wanted Roy to wait until the next day to make the trip, but he insisted he was feeling fine. Also, Jack and Maria were leaving the next day on a business trip, and wanted to complete the transaction before they left. It would be a full nine hours before Roy could possibly return. "Protect him, Lord," I whispered, as he pulled away from the house.

That afternoon, Tania and Nina came in from school. "Hi, Mom, how's Dad doing? Is he feeling O.K.?"

All day I had been telling myself that I would wait for Roy to return so we could give our children the news together, but I just couldn't wait.

"Dad's fine; and guess what? We're going to be able to buy the Marlowes' house!"

The girls looked at each other blankly. "What do you mean, Mom? Has someone bought our house in Pellston?"

As I explained to them about the telephone call from the Larimores, I realized what a wonderful opportunity this was to explain to our girls about an almighty God "who is able to do exceedingly abundantly above all that we ask or think" (Eph. 3:20).

Matt felt the excitement as he came into the house. Tania and Nina, both chattering at once, rushed to him to tell the news. His reaction was quick and to the point: "Oh, boy! A house of our own again!"

It was a tired, but jubilant Roy who came home that evening, waving the check at us as he walked in the door. Each of us had to inspect it, and wonder again at the goodness of God.

It was a subdued Kauppila family who sat at the supper table that night, seemingly drained of all emotion. We were thinking about the events of the last two days, and each was lost in his own thoughts.

Finally Roy spoke. "I want to say to my family that

yesterday, when God snatched me from certain death, it was a miracle. How I mixed up on my medication, I'll never know. The Lord was so good to allow me another chance to continue living. It made me realize just how much I love my family, and what each one means to me.

"At breakfast this morning, I told your mother how I thank God for the love and patience she has shown me during the time I've been so depressed, and I asked her forgiveness. She didn't think she had been that patient and loving, and wanted to ask my forgiveness. Then we both prayed, and asked God to forgive us and cleanse our hearts from bitterness, and to give us a new love for Him and for each other. I have asked God to make me the spiritual leader of this home, and be the spiritual example for my family that God wants me to be.

"Then was when the telephone rang. It was as if God were saying, 'I have had this miracle prepared for you, but I had to wait until you made your hearts right with each other, and with Me.'"

For Roy, that was a long speech. I was glad he had shared with our children what had happened. This would help them to learn firsthand how important it is for each one to keep himself clean before God, and with each other.

28

Home at Last

*

And we know that all things work together for good to
those who love God, to those who are the called according
to His purpose (Rom. 8:28).

Things began happening rapidly, like pieces of a puzzle
dropping into place. The check was deposited the following day, and Ted began completing the necessary paperwork.
The Marlowes had already been packing many of their
belongings into boxes. They were more than willing to give
us immediate possession.

The air of excitement in our home couldn't be squelched.
Our children were excited about the fact that they would
be returning to their former schools, and would be greeting all their old friends there. We would again be just a few
minutes from our church.

We had moved so often that we were beginning to feel
like professional movers. The difference this time was in
the excitement we were feeling. Our own home again! And
provided through such an unmistakable miracle of God!

When we actually had possession of our new home, we
began packing our belongings, and then moving them to
the new home, ready to be put away in their new locations.
As the twins and I worked together, Nina suddenly stopped
working, and said, "Mom, do you remember how Tania
and I cried so much when we first moved back to Royal
Oak?"

"Yes, honey; Mom remembers very, very well."

Nina continued, "We will always love it up north; but you know, Mom, moving down to Royal Oak was the best thing that could ever have happened to us. It wasn't easy to leave our friends up there. We didn't believe you when you said we would make new friends here. But we have."

Here Tania broke in, "Mom, when we began singing in the choir, becoming a part of the music program, and when we really began listening to the pastor teach the Bible, we could see why you and Dad love this church so much. And making new friends at church, and being involved with such super people as Gordy and Phyllis, having Bible studies with them, and, oh, just everything. We're really glad we're here."

"Tania, remember how excited we were when we started high school, and met some of the kids we'd gone to school with from kindergarten through the third grade, before we ever went up north?"

"Yeah! That was really neat."

I was so glad they had shared this with me. I knew from watching them that they were happy, but hearing them say it aloud made me especially glad.

Only a little over a month had gone by since we had received the special telephone call from Jack Larimore, and we were ready to do the final moving into our new home. It was time to go up north to bring down the rest of our belongings. Roy was again able to hire some boys to help him lift the remaining heavy articles into the truck. Then came the long drive back, returning late that night. For the second time, members of our beloved Sunday school class came to help Roy lift and place the heavy articles from the truck into our new home. Then they also helped do the heavy lifting of furniture from the Birmingham house and bring them into our new home.

This was a special day for us to remember, October 20,

1978, when we were again "home at last." As the days passed, we were occupied with settling in, until one day we discovered that we felt we really belonged there. Thank You, Lord!

By this time, I had worked in the new department of the hospital that I had been transferred to, for several months. My shoulder continued to bother me. It was well over a year since I had collided with that wall. Instead of improving, the pain in my shoulder had continued to increase. Finally my doctor shook his head. "I am putting you in the hospital for further tests, Tania. X-rays show nothing. Let's see what a different type of test will show."

That test report was to make it necessary for me to end my employment with the hospital. My doctor explained it to me:

"Tania, it is possible that you could further injure your shoulder, and completely lose the use of your arm. You should not be lifting at work, or at home. Surgery on this type of an injury is usually done within hours after it happens, to be effective. It is a torn rotator cuff."

There was no question about it then. My days of working outside the home were over. Would my family be sorry to have me at home again full time? I thought not! I had worked at the hospital for three years, and the Lord had used me there. I was grateful for that.

I began to think back over the many things that had happened to me in my lifetime. As a child, although I had no home, and very little food, I did have an abundance of love from my parents. I sometimes wondered, "Will I ever grow up? Will I ever be married and have children?" I knew one thing: I surely wanted them to have a different life than I had experienced.

Even in the hard places of my life, I could see God's watchful care. I began to think about the medical problems that I have: the faulty heart valve that behaves when I have ample rest and avoid undue stress; the ulcers that are controlled by medication; the glaucoma and migraines that are also treatable with medication. I am thankful to be close to the University of Michigan Hospital where doctors twice yearly keep a check on the growth on my optic nerve, and to hear them say that at present the growth is in remission. Truly the Lord has proved Himself able to provide ample grace in time of need.

The Lord has given us six wonderful children, the last three to the amazement of my doctor. It is a special blessing to me as I think of our precious family circle. Ours has been a close-knit family. Our children have grown up, never having had cousins, aunts, or uncles. (While Roy's parents were still living, they did have one set of grandparents.) It has been almost as if we have been an "orphan" family. We're all we've ever had.

Birthdays have been a special time for us to get together. I can still remember the surprise of finding out when my birthday was, and the bigger surprise I received in Kentucky when I learned that people celebrated birthdays! We make each birthday an important occasion, especially those of our only two grandchildren. Jennifer is ten, and her brother, Jeffrey, Jr., is four.

We see our "away-from-home" family frequently, and chat by telephone at least once or twice a week, in order to keep up with what is happening in their busy lives.

Krystina's husband, Doug, is busily involved with his own sales company. Krys is a customer service representative for one of the big auto companies, in the division that offers insurance coverage to its own employees. When I asked Krys what she does all day, she laughed and said, "That's easy to answer, I talk on the telephone. Actually, Mom, I enjoy it. I never know where the next call will come from, or what it will entail. It could be a local call, or from California, or Ohio, or wherever. Each call is a new challenge."

Lilly and her husband, Jeff, are the parents of Jennifer and Jeffrey. Our grandchildren are both "live wires," and know how to keep Nana and Grandpa hopping.

Jeff is a supervisor for an auto company. Lilly works in a medical clinic, a branch of a large local hospital in the area. Lilly describes her day in the following way: "What do I do? What *don't* I do? Wow! A little bit of everything. Receptionist, bookkeeper, billing, appointments, trying to keep everyone happy. And I love it."

Ruthie is a surgical technician at a large hospital. She assists in the operating room during open-heart and brain surgery, as well as other duties. I tried to watch a TV program showing an open-heart surgery being performed, but had to quit watching. "Yeah, Mom; you were watching what I watch every day. I guess you wouldn't want to have my job, would you?" I had to agree that I would not.

Each time I say to her, "Ruthie, when are you going to get married and give Mom some grandchildren?", she is quick to answer, "Until I'm very sure he is 'Mr. Right,' I sure don't want any man in my life." I am in complete agreement with her. I would not want any of my children to be married to a spouse not of God's choosing.

Tania and Nina are twenty years old, in their sophomore year of Bible college, majoring in psychology and evangelism. They have dedicated their lives to full-time Christian service, and have indicated that they are willing to go to a foreign mission field, should the Lord so lead.

When they were juniors in high school, they went with a teen work crew from our church to Guatemala, to help in the construction of a church building. Gordy and Phyllis went with the group, as well as Ben and Marty, our missionaries from Guatemala. Having this experience made a real impact on our twins. In tears, they said, "Mom, those people are destitute financially, but in spite of that they have such a love for the Lord that they put us to shame.

Compared to them, the *Norte Americanos* are millionaires. We have so much!" And then with a twinkle in their eyes, they added: "Yeah! Especially showers...did we ever miss being able to take a good hot shower when we cleaned up."

In the twins' senior year of high school, Gordy and Phyllis again were sponsors of a teen work crew, this time to Costa Rica. Those two trips out of the country have tenderized the twins' hearts to the needs of others, especially spiritual needs. We have been thankful for the emphasis and encouragement in missions projects. We are blessed to have missionaries in residence much of the time while they are on furlough who, along with Gordy and Phyllis and other adult sponsors, are willing to go with these young groups.

It is exciting for Roy and me to see our girls with the boys they date, seated around our kitchen table, studying the Bible together, and to hear them memorizing Scripture, or to observe them praying together.

Roy and I both "look up" to our sixteen-year-old Matt, who is already six feet, one inch. He is a junior in high school, and in a college preparatory course. Matt is our athlete, and enjoys playing on the church basketball team. No one cheers more loudly when he scores for his team than do his parents. However, we are equally pleased with his activity in the Campus Life Club at his school.

Roy has already counseled Matt in how to prepare for his life as an adult. "Matt, when you graduate from high school, you must train in two areas; first, Bible college training, to teach you how to be a Christian husband and father, and the spiritual leader in your home that God wants you to be. You must also train for a vocation, to prepare you to be able to provide for your family, when you get one."

Each year, Gordy and Phyllis take a group of high

school juniors and seniors on a "college tour" to allow the students to become acquainted with the Christian colleges in Michigan and neighboring states. This year Matt joined the group, and came back enthusiastic over the Christian college of his choice. "Oh, man! I've chosen where I want to go when I graduate from high school!"

Roy and I just looked at each other without saying a word. We could read each other's minds on this one, no words necessary. "Three in college at once? But how, Lord?"

We dearly love each of our children, our sons-in-law, and our grandchildren. Roy and I have given each one of them into the Lord's keeping. May His will be done in each of their lives, is our constant prayer.

Epilogue

✳

If God is for us, who can be against us? (Rom. 8:31).

As I think back over God's goodness to me, I remember especially one occasion when I was asked to speak at a Christian women's club in the Keweenaw Peninsula of Upper Michigan. When I arrived, the president of the club seemed upset, and was hesitant to tell me why. Finally she did: It seemed there was a woman who had arrived at the hotel before I did, who made it evident she was upset about my subject. She was antagonistic and belligerent, and determined to stay to hear me speak. She identified herself as a Communist sympathizer, and made the threat as she bought her ticket, "This speaker had better not say anything against Russia, or she'll wish she hadn't." She carried a suspicious-looking black case, and seated herself quite close to the speaker's table. The women in charge didn't quite know how to handle the situation, but one of them called her husband to come to the meeting in case of trouble.

When I heard the story, I let my imagination run wild. I had always wondered what I would do if I had to confront Communists again. I sometimes worried about my exposure of them every time I spoke. As I seated myself at the head table, the woman rose and came toward me. I managed a cheerful smile. "Hello, there," I said. "I'm glad to see you today." Then I promptly ducked my head down under the long white tablecloth as if to tie my shoe. I began to pray as never before. "God, this is Your day, and I am yours. Give me the right words to say, and still the fear in my heart. Help me to be willing to live for You, or to die for You!" Galatians 2:20 kept coming to mind: "I have been crucified with Christ; it is no longer I who live...."

When I raised my head, I saw that the woman's seat was empty. As I looked around to see where she might be, I saw her at the back door, getting a refund for her ticket. Then she left and did not return. After I was introduced, I rose and again told some of the story recorded in this book. I told how God had kept me from starving in Russia; how He kept me from dying in a concentration camp; how He delivered me during the disaster of a problem marriage; how He led me to know Him who had been seeking me all my life. As I spoke, the realization flooded over me, that the same God who had done all this, had protected me again that very day. He could surely be trusted to see me through the seemingly overwhelming problems I would face in the future! He would bring me through them all triumphantly, and when He at last called me home to heaven I would be able to thank Him, face to face.

My mind went back to that day years before, when as a child not yet twelve years old, I stood in the circle of my father's arms, surrounded by the other prisoners, the German guards, the sounds of the city of Kiev, and the waiting train, and heard him plead, "Meet me in heaven, Tatyana Pavlovna, my own little Tania!" Now I could bow my head, years later, and whisper the answer, "I'm coming, Father! By God's grace, I'll meet you there!"